Jesus Loves Brixton Too

Jesus Loves Brixton Too

MICHAEL ARMITAGE

Marshall Pickering

Marshall Morgan and Scott
Marshall Pickering
3 Beggarwood Lane, Basingstoke, Hants RG23 7LP, UK

Copyright © 1986 by Michael Armitage

First published in 1986 by
Marshall Morgan and Scott Publications Ltd
Part of the Marshall Pickering Holdings Group
A subsidiary of the Zondervan Corporation

ISBN 0 551 013400

Text set in Times by
Brian Robinson, Buckingham.
Printed in Great Britain by
Anchor Brendon Ltd, Tiptree, Essex.

Contents

Introduction

Jesus and the Inner City

Our inner city areas are rarely out of the news. They are the places where many people put down their first roots, where immigration begins, where ghettos are made, where extended family systems of centuries' duration have been broken up, where the guts of old communities have been torn out and modern material transplants made. Unfortunately the transplants are often rejected by the host cities, and the body of the city as a whole suffers. A trip through Newcastle, Manchester, Liverpool or Birmingham should be enough to endorse this point. London seems not to have suffered so badly—but its Victorian suburbs which have now been absorbed into the urban sprawl are areas of major replanning where riots have taken place.

Brixton is one of those areas where fine Victorian properties were allowed to fester and decay for decades until expensive plans for high density estates were drawn up. My parish has more than its fair share of them. There are actually no fewer than six housing estates in my parish alone, and one of them, the Angell Town Estate, has the highest density of population in Europe!

The mixed inner city populations suffer from massive unemployment, deprivation, and alienation as well as bad housing. All of this, together with institutionalised racism, was singled out for attention by Lord Scarman in his report following the 1981 countrywide riots. By 1986 things, far from improving, have actually got worse and there have been more riots. It is on all of our consciences that little or nothing has happened as a result of Lord

Scarman's careful and probing conclusions. Indeed the business of 'rate-capping' has meant that while the government has given £12 million to Lambeth through the Urban Partnership schemes during the last year, the government has taken back £19 million through rate-capping. 'To him who has shall more be given and to him who has not, even what he has shall be taken away.' (Matt. 13:12)

In Brixton one of the areas of major deprivation and decay was heavily vandalised during the 1981 riots. It was the main centre of drugs dealing in Brixton and had numerous small illegal after-hours drinking, dominoes and reggae clubs. But it also afforded cheap and nourishing food in small cafés, craft shops, and shops specialising in West Indian records, foods and clothing. It also provided deep, soundproof cellars where the loud reggae noises were contained better than they ever could be on the modern estates. It has now been demolished.

Part of this area, which afforded the flashpoint for the earlier riots, was situated at the heart of my parish and was known locally as the Front Line. It has now been demolished—but 'Living on the Frontline' survives, not only in the Eddy Grant song of the same name. It is still a reality for many who live in Brixton. Because they have little money, they are always the first to experience the effects of any minute changes in the government's economic, legal or welfare policies.

Living in Brixton requires a revolutionary state of mind. It also requires a massive sensitivity to people's needs. Many of these needs will be obvious—but many are more subtle. Not only do you need to be sensitive to the needs of those who are hungry, poor, badly housed, or trapped by their physical situations, but you also need to become aware of the mental frustrations, the forced dependencies, and the way in which initiative and creativity are stifled by the overwhelming pressures of sheer existence.

Living in Brixton means living in poverty. Fashionable shops have closed and moved out. Even Tesco's has the smallest selection of the cheapest lines, compared with any other store in the country. Smaller shops regularly go out of business. There is no money in Brixton.

Living in Brixton means living in one room in bed and breakfast temporary accommodation for years, living in overcrowded conditions, living in estates which leave people vulnerable to burglary and at risk from muggers. It also means living in large families, often with only one parent.

Living in Brixton means being unemployed—its unemployment rate is one of the highest in Europe—and that means living on Social Security and Supplementary Benefit, pleading for extra money for bedding or to buy new shoes for the children. If you are old it means the sudden cessation of pension payments for no reason, and going hungry until payments are restored; if you are young it means that you have no future and that you may never be able to earn your own living.

Living in Brixton means being black for at least half the population. Being black in Britain means being asked where you come from even if you were born here. It means finding that all job vacancies are already filled. It means being treated as a criminal—guilty without trial, with no chance of proving your own innocence. It also means *not* being a policeman, a banker, a stockbroker, a judge or an MP.

Living in Brixton means that you have done something wrong. All figures of authority from the most humble DHSS officer up to the Prime Minister, believe that you are potentially dangerous.

Living in Brixton means that you are numbered among common criminals, drugs dealers, pimps, prostitutes, rioters, muggers. Because you live with and mix with the wrong people, it is bound to rub off on you sooner or later.

Living in Brixton means biting your tongue each time you are treated unjustly; as you are stopped and searched in the street; as you are flung into a police cell for doing nothing wrong; as a septuagenarian judge, who knows nothing about you, your background or your lifestyle, gives you a prison sentence for a first offence; as your children are taken from you because your husband is in prison and you can't cope; as you become yet another statistic of deprivation and poverty to be ignored by a compassionless government.

Living in Brixton means being often in the news, on television or in newspaper headlines, and always being condemned.

Living in Brixton means struggling to bring your children up decently, always hoping for the best and doing all you can to improve things, trying to help other people, yet always being frustrated, repressed and struggling with failure.

Living in Brixton means praying a lot in the knowledge that others are praying too. It also means enjoying rich and varied worship and trying to work out what it means to be a Christian in a practical way.

And then living in Brixton means living in the middle of a world microcosm, a healthy, heaving centre of life, laughter and world culture. Living in Brixton means pioneering community arts involving theatre, music, education, leisure and all the help people freely give.

Living in Brixton has amazing potential if we are given financial and other help, and a small amount of encouragement.

Jesus did not live in Brixton, but the city exerted a fatal fascination for him. It was in the city of Jerusalem that Jesus identified himself so fully with those at the bottom of the heap that his message still rings clear and true to those who live in Brixton today. His championship of the poor and needy was to lead to his death. Would it still happen today?

Trying to answer that question and trying to discover why it was that someone as good, kind and helpful as Jesus was executed as a criminal, has led me to write this study after thirteen years as a vicar in Brixton.

In order to explore Christianity in this way, a belief in the complete humanity of Jesus is presupposed. This is the heart of Christianity which makes it different from every other religion. Our God cared so much about us all that he was prepared to live with us and to identify with us, to bear all the pains we have to suffer, and even to die a particularly painful and ignominious death. It was through the resurrection that we came to believe that

Jesus was, in fact, God; and, with the benefit of hindsight we are able to re-evaluate the records of his life and teachings which have been handed down to us from the earliest Christians.

There can be many possible interpretations of the person Jesus we find in the gospels. The one I see, with my Brixton eyes, is not the image of Jesus found in popular films. Once when I was presenting a BBC TV Songs of Praise programme, I interviewed a sculptor whose faith had led him to portray significantly different images of Jesus in his work. He was in fact a priest, but his telling images of the joy and the suffering of Jesus were found in the clown and the scarecrow in various expressive forms. This shook some people's faith and we received several letters of complaint. More importantly though, we got many more letters from people who had found a powerful theology and inspiration in a Jesus who both encompasses and supercedes such images.

The person of Jesus I find in the gospels is a man of the people, with wit, intelligence, sensitivity, compassion and, above all, a concern to share his ideas about God, people and the world with those who will listen. This Jesus is a hero and one you could hope to model yourself on. His example is not an unattainable ideal. But this is also a Jesus who threatened people, who made life uncomfortable for the rich, and who identified with the poor and needy. He overturned many accepted values and revealed a way of life we all could follow which would change the world, revolutionising the way we relate to each other and to society. This Jesus is relevant here and now, yet, since his Christianity is a complete way of life, not just a Sunday hobby, he is a potential threat to political leaders and all those in authority.

In this book I shall try to share my view of the Jesus who fascinated and challenged the people of his day; the Jesus whose personality and charisma attracted so many followers; the Jesus who started a movement which is still growing in strength. I shall also try to reveal a practical Jesus who requires us to live his kind of life and shows us how. This is a Jesus who expects us to express our love for each other in a practical everyday way, simply as a response to God's love for us all:

> 'When I was hungry you gave me food, when thirsty you gave me drink; when I was a stranger, you took me into your home, when naked you clothed me; when I was ill you came to my help, when in prison you visited me'. (Matt. 25:35, 36)

This precise identification of Jesus with the poor, the deprived, the oppressed and the powerless gives all those who live in the inner city hope and challenges all those who do not to act in a practical Christian way. Doing this would bring about a Christian revolution. I believe that, as followers of Jesus, we need to love and care for the city, as Jesus did.

1

Jesus Was A Revolutionary

Theologians don't know what they're talking about. This is not intended to be a controversial statement, so I hope that theologians have a sense of humour! In fact it is meant to be a definition. Since none of us knows God, and by definition he is unknowable as well as being all powerful, all knowing and infinite, no matter how much we write or say about him, essentially none of us knows what we are writing or talking about—even those who have dedicated their lives to describing the indescribable. Nevertheless, impossible or not, this doesn't stop people, theologians or otherwise, from trying to talk or write about God.

Similarly we cannot prove that God exists—though many people have tried. It is inevitable, however, that anyone who has asked that first important searching religious question, 'What is life about?' must consider the existence of God among other atheistic and humanistic answers.

Luckily we are all different and these kinds of philosophical speculations are not the preoccupation of everyone. There are many people who feel that too much analysis, whether of God or the Bible, begins to devalue their faith.

I have friends who cannot see a car without wanting to get under the bonnet and start pulling it all to bits to see how it works. There are many people like that in Brixton: garages are an epidemic and car repairs a major industry, sport and hobby! These people have a similar state of mind to that of the analysers of religious belief. But, just as many people are never able to put their car back together again, so many people remain unimpressed by religious 'proofs' which don't work for them or are too difficult to understand.

I'm the kind of person who just likes to get into a car and drive away. I don't really care how it works nor do I want to know—I can leave that to the experts—just as long as it *does* work. I think that, for many people, belief in God is rather like that. As an idea, as a concept, it works, especially in helping us to understand what life is about, and it can inspire us to greater things as people. This is true of all the major religions of the world which hold to a belief in God.

But, for Christians, if belief in God answers questions for us, inspires us and makes demands on us, how much more must belief in Christ? This is what makes us distinctively Christian: we believe that all the things Jesus said and did as recorded in St Paul's letters and in the Gospels are there for us to follow and to learn from in a practical way in order to become his disciples. More than that, they make demands on us and require us to relate with and help other people.

I believe that trying to live the kind of life that Jesus wants requires Christians to take on extra responsibilities. It is not just a matter of an individual person's search for God, a personal challenge, or even seeking out the company of like-minded people. It involves, more broadly, a life shared by us all in a Christian community—what I suppose we should now call a total lifestyle.

It seems to me that Jesus wanted to establish such a lifestyle in a way so dynamic and powerful that he expected it to develop into a kind of heaven on earth. And this is, I believe, the true force of the words in his most famous prayer: 'Your kingdom come on earth as in heaven'. This idea underlies his various sayings about the Kingdom.

In this Jesus was revolutionary. His Jewish background, on the other hand, was fairly traditional. Even though much of his teaching is grounded in the Hebrew scriptures, he was asking people then, and he challenges us now, to evaluate that background afresh and to prune away redundant traditions and clutter which have served to obscure ideas about God and the ways he has been seen to act in history.

Jesus begins his ministry, according to the Gospel of Mark, with a memorable saying; his message is clear and forceful, though far from simple:

The time has come; the Kingdom of God is upon you; repent, and believe the Gospel (Mark 1:15).

It is the urgency of this message that makes its impact on me. 'The time has come'—NOW is the time for action. And yet two thousand years later we're still waiting for the decisive moment rather like some eternal committee meeting! Jesus' message remains direct and emphatic and it challenges us to action. In this it can be seen that Jesus was not proclaiming a once and for all moment in history. Those words call for an active response each time we read or hear them, and a reassessment of the effectiveness of our Christian lives before God. Yet at the same time the urgency must remain. This tension was present for the early church. Many of Jesus' followers believed that the world was about to end during the period following the crucifixion. St Paul writes:

'For this we tell you as the Lord's word: we who are left alive until the Lord comes shall not forestall those who have died; because at the word of command, at the sound of the archangel's voice and God's trumpet call, the Lord himself will descend from heaven; first the Christian dead will rise, then we who are left alive shall join them, caught up in clouds to meet the Lord in the air'. (1 Thess. 4:15)

Much of this comes from traditional Jewish teaching, but this almost apocalyptic expectation is not fulfilled and Paul's attitude changes as the world continues to exist.

Jesus challenges us with urgency—but he also challenges us with opportunity. Giving us the time to act forces us to accept responsibility for that action, and for making the most of our God-given opportunity. The significance of the time is that it gives us the urgent opportunity to act to remove the outrage of human suffering and injustice which needs to be eradicated from God's world.

The next words in Mark have caused libraries to be written about their right interpretation, and yet the statement seems at first sight to be self-evident: 'The Kingdom of God is upon you' (Mark 1:15).

Once more the urgency is underlined, the Kingdom of God is here and now with us, but what does that mean and what is this 'Kingdom'?

The theological background is complicated and is usually covered by the term 'eschatology' which has to do with the Last Things at the end of time. In this way the Kingdom could be seen as something in the future and, taken with its parallel expression 'the Kingdom of Heaven', something in heaven, that is, after death. This was a prevailing Victorian thought as we know from the sacred songs and solos about little match girls and flowersellers whose death wafts their innocent souls prematurely into heaven, like 'Underneath the Gaslight's Glitter' and Piccolomini's 'Ora Pro Nobis'. Here are two examples from Sankey's original edition of 'Sacred Songs and Solos':

No 371

> When the dewy light was fading,
> And the sky in beauty smiled,
> Came a whisper, like an echo,
> From a pale and dying child:
> 'Mother, in that golden region,
> With its pearly gates so fair,
> Up among the happy angels,
> Is there room for Mary there?'

No 415:

> 'I should like to die,' said Willie, 'if my papa could die too;
> But he says he isn't ready, 'cause he has so much to do;
> And my little sister Nellie says that I must surely die,
> And that she and mamma—then she stopp'd, because it made me cry.'

A hundred years ago these sentiments are said to have 'reduced the population of Hell by a million souls'. Moody and Sankey were evangelising the inner city areas in the late decades of the last century just as Wesley had evangelised those who worked in Blake's 'dark satanic mills' a century earlier. But there was little hope for the inner city working classes this side of death: the pains of this life were to be endured until we could all be in heaven with the angels, like those in our stained glass windows, making heavenly music into eternity.

C.H. Dodd was one of those who put the cat among the pigeons, developing Albert Schweitzer's early twentieth century theories, with his concept of 'realised eschatology'. By this Dodd meant that the true significance of the Kingdom is that it is here and now, and not something that belongs to some unspecified future. Jesus' message was that we should act now, using every opportunity to bring about justice and redress what is wrong. These are the signs of the Kingdom.

Using this concept, Mediaeval and Victorian ideas about enduring this 'naughty world' and looking for some blissful fulfilment after death, fail to grasp the point that Jesus is the Lord of the Here and Now at least as much as the Future. The idea of enduring this life in hope of the next helped to maintain the feudal system and also served to contain the working classes in the last century. But it is contrary to the ways of Jesus.

Is it possible, then, that the Kingdom, rather like the Empire, is an outdated anachronistic concept? Although we still have a monarch in Britain, not many other countries do, and even our Queen does not have much, if any, executive power—the royal assent seems more like a rubber stamp. The notion of an Absolute Monarch is now lost to history except for such vestiges that remain in dictatorial states like Amin's Uganda. From this one may well conclude that a 'Kingdom' is not an idea we can easily comprehend today. But a Kingdom in this sense is not what Jesus was actually talking about. His kingdom is probably better represented by the earlier discussion of community and lifestyle. The difficulty is caused by language and comprehension, and it hinges on the word translated as 'Kingdom'. The word in Mark's Gospel was originally in Greek, but it has a background in the language Jesus actually spoke—which was Aramaic—and in the Hebrew with which he was familiar as a Jew. In each case and in each language our word Kingdom is inadequate to express the thought world evoked by this word. The point is that the Kingdom does not refer to some kind of finite country nor to a group of subject people. In fact the word refers to the actual act of ruling in the sense of having responsibility for calling together a community with a common allegiance—in this case, to Jesus.

The group Jesus gathered was initially small, though it grew quickly. His followers had in common an allegiance to Jesus, a dependence on him, a sharing of his view of God and a sharing of his understanding of the needs of other people, and how to help them. Jesus was calling together a community who were dedicated to share a way of life that was shown to them by Jesus. This is what Jesus meant by the Kingdom. An individual response to Jesus' teaching is therefore inadequate because from the call of the disciples it is clear that Jesus expected a shared and collective response.

As Christianity has spread the Kingdom has come to mean the whole of our society, the whole world or, small local communities trying to live a life that follows Jesus. The Kingdom could obviously refer to 'the Church', but that is not a word used in the gospels—it belongs to Paul alone—and it begs two thousand years worth of different meanings! If we can see the Kingdom as referring to Christian communities, and to *us, here* and *now*, our whole way of thinking about Christianity will be challenged.

The next word that Jesus uses is one that develops this understanding of the Kingdom. It is one of our most familiar Christian words and also one of the most difficult: 'Repent'.

It is traditional Christian language to tell people to repent of their sins, but the development of psychology and counselling, particularly during the last forty years, has taught people to think differently. We are now learning that an over-emphasis on guilt feelings can be counterproductive especially if it leaves people grovelling in a mire of self disgust and guilt which is not only masochistic but almost addictive. In past ages the Church has exploited such feelings as we know not least from the mediaeval processions of flagellantes and the self-punishment suffered by pilgrims.

The kind of repentence Jesus meant was not this, however, and its true meaning bridges the ages with its continued relevance. Jesus was talking of a return to God, in a radical sense, involving a change of mind, of heart, and of our whole outlook, bringing a healing sense of renewal. He wanted us to turn around completely—and this is the main meaning of the Greek word translated as 'repent'. But I believe that an even greater significance may be found when it is appreciated that a synonym for 'turning around' is 'revolution'. I believe that Jesus intended to cause a revolution in all of us that would involve all of us. He wanted us not only to change society so as to make it God's community imbued with Jesus' own lifestyle, but also to change the world. To this end he established his group of twelve and commissioned them to tell the good news to the whole world:

'With these things the birth pangs of the new age begin. As for you, be on your guard. You will be handed over to the courts. You will be flogged in synagogues. You will be summoned to appear before governors and kings on my account to testify in their presence. But before the end the Gospel must be proclaimed to all nations'. (Mark 13:8)

'Before the end' means literally 'first'. Jesus' revolution begins with taking the gospel to the world and once more we are challenged to continue this work with urgency.

The last part of the proclamation says, 'And believe in the gospel'. Yet again words that seem simple and familiar can cause great difficulties as we struggle to discover their exact meanings. Belief, like faith, is impossible to define but it carries an important sense of being in a right relationship with God. This presupposes that we ourselves have to make an effort to approach God and to find out what the Gospel means.

The familiar definition of 'The Gospel' is the Good News. We take it to mean the whole story of Jesus—but

Mark cannot have expected that Jesus meant this at the very start of his ministry. The Good News Jesus actually proclaimed can be found in the first sermon that he preached in his home town (Luke 4:18 & 19). His text was taken from Isaiah 61 and speaks of good news for the poor, the release of prisoners, the recovery of sight for the blind, the freeing of broken victims and the proclamation of the Jubilee year. This is a message of hope which links the aspirations of the Hebrew exiles in ancient Babylon, who were looking forward to their return and the joy and liberation of their Jubilee celebration, with the hopes of the early Christians for the liberating joy of their Jesus movement. It shows that Mark believed that Jesus was inaugurating a new age, (Mark 13:8) involving a renewed relationship with God and a closer relationship with each other. Perhaps Jesus himself was conscious of starting a movement which would mark the beginning of what we may now call the Christian era. Whether Jesus had such a notion or not it is clear that Mark was convinced of it and emphasises this sense of a new beginning with words of Jesus which sound almost like a revolutionary manifesto when their full potential is evaluated. But, however revolutionary that first small community of Christians may have been, what eventually resulted from it is the Church as we know it.

What would Jesus make of this institution which has come such a long way from that small, vital and exciting group he formed with his twelve friends? Would he be delighted by our great worship places, our complicated theology, our pomp and ceremony, our church services? Would he feel that the movement had grown and developed beyond his wildest dreams, or, alternatively, would he wonder where it had all gone wrong? How could all of this have grown from the down-to-earth sharing and struggling of those few people all those years ago? How could all of this have developed from that first revolutionary proclamation?

People usually assess the success of a church by the number of people who attend. Churches singled out as good examples are usually those with large congregations, a high rate of giving, and numerous people involved in a myriad of church organisations. These churches not only pay their way, they also manage to pay out large amounts of money to their diocese to help other improverished churches. These successful churches are found mainly, though not exclusively, in the suburbs, in commuterland. They are rarely to be found in the inner city but if they are it is usually because they have developed some kind of specialised ministry, such as a charismatic ethos or an extreme anglo-catholicism, which attracts people from far and wide. Successful churches are usually able to cope well with committee structures and with highly organised parish councils, deanery synods, diocesan synods and the like. Their members are good at proposing motions, amendments to amendments, and voting on them, electing secretaries, treasurers and subcommittees, taking minutes, keeping diaries and controlling finances with the most astute investments. They are so well organised that they are ideal for training people in the formal middle class structures of the Church of England. In fact most of our parishes are like this, or aspire to be, and it is from these parishes that the majority of our ordinands come, and the people who serve on all our diocesan boards and committees.

These successful parishes are admirable—they are beautifully kept, everyone has their little job to do, and the vicar is well supported. In fact many of these parishes could do perfectly well without a vicar. They are inevitably seen as good training grounds for curates who are sure to learn the ropes quickly in such efficiently run parishes.

This is the success story of the suburban church. The story is not the same in the cities, however. In the city, and in speaking about the city I shall speak mainly about Brixton because that is the inner city area I know best, there is not a thriving middle class population who go to work in the city each day. Instead there are unemployed people, lots of unemployed people. In my parish at least half the people are unemployed. The norm is not mum, dad, 2·5 children and dog Spot. At least a third of our families have only one parent with up to six children. There are also a lot of old people. Not those who have retired with a nice little nest egg to see out their last days, and who have all kinds of gifts to offer the community with their extra time. No, the old people I speak of are on basic pensions, they have had nothing all their lives, will never own their own home and barely have even a bed to sleep on.

I know all this because I have lived and worked in both kinds of parishes and have experienced the differences between inner and outer parishes myself. I think I can best illustrate the difference with one little story.

I am the chairman of a small local charity called the Brixton Dispensary. It was originally intended for those in need of medical help who could not afford it—but it has developed a wonderful tradition of giving small handouts to the needy at Christmas. The local vicars and church people let us know of the people who won't be having much of a Christmas and we are able to give them hampers or something similar. I took a hamper round to an old couple in my parish last Christmas and they were overwhelmed. With tears in her eyes the old lady told me that her larder had never been so full (they have no fridge) but I'd really only taken them a few basic foodstuffs: tea, butter, sugar, a small cake, a pudding and some jam and tinned meat as extras. I hope that this one example begins to show up some of the differences between inner and outer parishes.

Many of our inner city people are not used to committee structures. They are not often even aware of their rights as tenants of council property, and they find it embarrassing to approach or use many of the various helping agencies available. They are intimidated by authority and are frustrated by bureaucratic structures. Small wonder that so few of them feature among those in the church's hierarchy. But, then, the church has never really tried to meet them where they are, or sought alternative structures which could actually include them. There are people in my congregation who still remember how the servants used to sit upstairs in the gallery so that they would not mix with the posh people downstairs. Needless to say this was in the days when Brixton itself was a rich suburb!

Another feature of inner city areas is their constantly shifting populations. Once the old communities and family groupings were broken up it became impossible to build communities again. People move in and out and rarely put down roots. As fast as you get to know your congregation, one prominent family moves away, and you have to start all over again. It is also significant that in our inner city areas we have a greater mix of people from the Commonwealth and other parts of the world. When you read St Peter's speech in Acts 2 it may cross your mind that the inner city area of Jerusalem was a bit like Brixton with all those people from all over the then known world gathered there. And this brings me round to answering one of my earlier questions. Jesus might well feel more at home in our chaotic inner city churches with their failing mixed congregations than in the well-ordered successful parishes of the outer areas. I believe that Jesus always directs our attention to the poor and needy and that he would find in the problems of the inner cities, fertile soil in which to sow the seeds of his Kingdom. These are the areas where his message can take root and grow, bringing about the revolution he initiated long ago but which still has not changed the world as he would have wanted.

If Jesus' message was truly revolutionary, it has many more implications for Christians than we have yet realised, with its powerful and liberating message. Jesus challenges us both individually and collectively in ways we can scarcely cope with, protected as we are and lulled into a false sense of security by our institutionalised worship and church structures. The main significance of Jesus' message, however, is for Christians in our inner cities who are not part of life's success story and who need his help to free themselves from the injustices which determine their abilities and initiatives. I believe that Jesus challenges all those in a stronger position to help the ones who are less privileged and to bring about a more equal sharing of resources, in the deprived areas of both this country and of the world.

'Christian Poverty does not mean penury. It does not mean starvation and homelessness. These are not virtues, but evils to be resisted and destroyed.'
Archbishop of Canterbury, Calcutta, Ash Wednesday 1986.

2

Jesus Was Poor

Jesus' identification with, and care for, the poor is endorsed in Luke at the beginning of his ministry when he goes to preach in Nazareth. He reads the jubilee proclamation of Isaiah, and not only gets thrown out of town for his pains but almost killed!

'So he came to Nazareth, where he had been brought up, and went to synagogue on the Sabbath day as he regularly did. He stood up to read the lesson and was handed the scroll of the prophet Isaiah. He opened the scroll and found the passage which says,

> "The spirit of the Lord is upon me because he has anointed me;
> he has sent me to announce good news to the poor,
> to proclaim release for prisoners and recovery of sight for the blind;
> to let the broken victims go free,
> to proclaim the year of the Lord's favour."

He rolled up the scroll, gave it back to the attendant, and sat down: and all eyes in the synagogue were fixed on him. He began to speak: "Today," he said, "this text which you have just heard has come true." At these words the whole congregation were infuriated. They leapt up, threw him out of the town, and took him to the brow of the hill on which it was built, meaning to hurl him over the edge. But he walked straight through them all, and went away.' (Luke 4:16)

If we as Christians are to take these words in a literal sense, as I believe we ought, then we must all work to secure the release of prisoners in, say, Brixton prison. Most of the prisoners there are on remand and so by British law are innocent anyway. But just to consider such a move would make any one of us sound insane. This may well leave us open to the charge that we don't take the gospel seriously enough, and that we lack the courage of our Christian convictions. Many Christians try to bridge this gap by doing work which reveals a sincere care and concern for prisoners, without actively working to do away with prisons. There are very useful prison visiting schemes, and bodies which help prisoners' families, and prisoners themselves after release.

I have taken instrumental groups into Brixton prison to perform folk masses and lead singsongs. I have visited parishioners of mine in almost every prison in the country. The feeling I am left with is that this kind of good work, while totally valid, is in fact an inadequate response to Jesus' challenge to totally revolutionise our penal system and dispose of prison as a method of dealing with the problems of our society.

Why is it that we cannot act literally as our gospels ask us to? Are we too frightened or are we too comfortable? Or do we interpret it all away in some vague 'spiritual' sense and pretend that it's all meant for somebody else?

Jesus makes considerable demands on us but our reaction is to turn away rather than to turn around and repent. His earliest hearers found it difficult enough, but to those in the middle classes who are better placed and have more resources to help the poor, Jesus is preaching revolution.

There are various levels at which we can act and speak in considering fair shares and social justice. The Sermon on the Mount offers two of these in the different interpretations in Matthew's and Luke's gospels. Some people believe that Jesus is describing an ethical system for a heavenly Kingdom. But if, as I have been arguing, the Kingdom, the community Jesus inaugurated, is being established here and now, then we ought to be sharing social ideas, religious ideas and moral notions for the Christian community to be living out now. The Beatitudes in Matthew seem to be proposing ethics for the future

Kingdom while the version in Luke seems to be encouraging active work in the community now. Compare Matthew,

> 'How blest are those who know their need of God;
> the Kingdom of Heaven is theirs.' (Matt. 5:3)
> 'How blest are those who hunger and thirst to see right prevail; they shall be satisfied.' (Matt. 5:6)

with Luke:

> 'How blest are you who are in need; the Kingdom of God is yours.
> How blest are you who now go hungry; your hunger will be satisfied.' (Luke 6:20, 21)

New Testament scholars, in trying to work out just what Jesus' original words might have been usually try to take either the form of the saying with fewest words and embellishments (if the saying is found in several gospels), or they take the reading which, at face value, is the most difficult in the context. This is based on two assumptions: first, the gospel writer may add words to make Jesus' sayings seem easier to understand, but he is unlikely to leave out words Jesus may actually have spoken. Secondly, if a saying doesn't quite fit its context, feels awkward, or is hard to understand, the more difficult reading is perhaps nearer to the words Jesus actually spoke since the pressure on the gospel writer will always be to make things fit into place as neatly as possible.

The gospel writers would want to preserve all the words of Jesus they could find, so it is unlikely that they would deliberately leave any out. However, if they found a longer version they would inevitably record the longer version. Suppose I use a more familiar version of the first Beatitude. Matthew has 'Blessed are the poor in Spirit', while Luke has 'Blessed are the poor'. It seems most unlikely to me that Luke would deliberately have left out 'in Spirit', so I assume that Matthew's source had a different, longer version of the saying. The trouble is that the longer version loses the characteristic simplicity and forthrightness we normally associate with the sayings of Jesus. In other words it is more likely that Jesus' true challenge was in the words of Luke—and it follows that those who prefer Matthew's more cushioned version, taking the saying out of the practical social sphere, are ducking the issue.

There are other passages which support this case. In spite of Matthew's apparent watering down of Luke's more challenging formulation, his version of an encounter with a wealthy young man puts the whole matter of identifying with the poor into a revolutionary perspective. The story is found, identical almost word for word, in both Mark and Luke.

> 'Jesus said, "If you wish to go the whole way, go, sell your possessions and give to the poor, and then you will have riches in heaven, and come, follow me".' (Matt. 19:21, Mark 10:21, Luke 18:22)

Mark adds a characteristic personal observation: 'At these words his face fell and he went away with a heavy heart; for he was a man of great wealth.'

Many people would argue that they do their bit for charity, that individually they give as much as they can, as well as looking after their own families. Jesus does not offer much support for family loyalty. In fact he seems to believe that the urgency of the situation requires a concern for people which goes far beyond the family. 'Who is my mother? Who are my brothers?' (Mark 3:33)—he asks when he is told that his family is outside, and goes on to describe *everyone* present as his mother and brothers. On another occasion, one of his disciples wants to go to his father's funeral but Jesus' uncompromising reply is: 'Follow me and leave the dead to bury their dead.' (Matt. 8:22)

Although he supports charitable giving, Jesus actually says, 'Sell *all* you have, and give to the poor'. This seems to me to be a far-reaching and very unsettling attack, not just on middle class life, but on any way of life that does not completely upset current values in order to discriminate positively for the poor and needy. This is the heart of his religion. It is what God demands of us all and Jesus expects all Christians to shake up the present order and join in his revolution.

In the inner city we are forced into Jesus' way of thinking because we are surrounded by so much need. Our world order is already inverted.

What would happen if we were all to do this? Presumably if we sold everything and gave to the poor, we'd become the poor ourselves. We must remember that Jesus' message is to a society in which the gulf between the rich and the poor is a huge one. His reaction to social justice is very different from that of our government today. Quite clearly Jesus was not a monetarist! His challenge would eventually lead to a more equitable sharing of resources.

The fact is that the poor, the deprived and those least able to protect themselves against inhuman policies are found crammed together in our inner cities. Within a half mile radius of my church, for instance, there are about 30,000 people living in an area of central Brixton which, according to the 1981 census, has a density of population three times higher than even the London average. The census also disclosed that at least one third of the Borough of Lambeth's households had incomes on or below the 'official' poverty line. The position has worsened in the intervening years as unemployment has continued to increase and the government has cut financial support. At the present time nearly two-thirds of all households in Lambeth claim supplementary benefit. It is almost impossible to cope with deprivation on a scale like this. For Christians in Brixton it is a constant problem maintaining the energy and know-how to be able to offer the people in our care some help as they are manipulated and violated daily by the political and economic forces in our society. The tragic cases of child beating are a symptom of all this. While they can in no way be excused, people who feel utterly powerless and genuinely frustrated in every effort to improve their conditions, do sometimes take it out on those who are even more dependent and powerless than themselves.

If you live in one of the small towns or villages of the outer parishes it is almost impossible to understand this state of affairs, because in these areas there is a societal set up which is traditional and has worked for centuries all over the world. I shall call it the village model. In the village model you have the local chief, maybe the squire, the parson, the publican, the doctor, the teacher, the butcher, the baker, the postman, the rich, the poor and so on. Everyone has his or her place. Each is dependent on the other and this binds them all into a cohesive community which will even cope with those who commute in and out during the week. This system prevents the terrible alienation people experience when they are forced into ad hoc 'communities' in the inner city. London's post-war planning policies, and those in particular which have raped Brixton, have created enormous problems for people trying to make a home in the area.

The village model itself, while it probably remains in the backs of our minds, is irrelevant in these replanned areas—and yet no other positive model has yet emerged to take its place. This means that people never feel settled, nor can they find their own niche in a constantly changing and insecure environment.

The population of my parish, for instance, is made up of young families, single parent families and old people—the poor and the powerless—not to mention the unemployed. They have no 'disposable income' and find it impossible to make both ends meet, especially as fuel bills and prescription charges keep increasing. Local charities and social services regularly get requests for help from people who cannot meet their gas, electricity or telephone bills. Yet old people and young children must have adequate heating in order to survive—they are the groups most vulnerable to health risks—and old people are at risk without a telephone to break their isolation or to summon help if they have an accident.

A clear sign of poverty has been that, over the past four or five years, in the once flourishing shopping centre of Brixton many major shops have closed down: Bon Marche (John Lewis), Littlewoods, John Collier, C&A, the Co-op, Pride and Clark and Wades, as well as several local jewellers, restaurants and delicatessens. Even Tesco's carry the most restricted lines I have ever seen in their shops.

The riots and rates are partly responsible for this, but the main culprit is plain poverty. In Brixton the pool rooms, the gyms, the pubs, the cafés and similar places where people meet are empty on Tuesdays and Wednesdays because people don't get their DHSS payments until Thursday or Friday! It is a way of life. If you manage to get a credit card, it merely stores up major problems for the future.

There remain only a handful of professional people who can sign passports and the like, the clergy being the only ones who live on the job! There are no young professionals with social consciences or with the time or money to enrich our community.

The inner city areas are the thin end of the wedge. They need more resources because they have a greater concentration of the population who need and will use more resources of any kind—especially money. They also have the highest proportion of the poorest people. It is precisely these people who will feel the first effects of any adverse trade balance or recession of the economy as a whole. The government should undoubtedly do more to help, but it is entangled in its own policies and lack of compassion for those in need.

Consider the following equation: the British taxpayer pays something like £3,000,000 each day to protect and service the people on the Falkland Islands. There are about 2,000 people living there. There are about 20,000 people living in my parish alone: ten times more! Just imagine what that kind of injection of financial support could do for the people of Brixton, for their living conditions and quality of life. And yet at the present time the government is cutting even the financial aid we had. I believe that Jesus is the champion of poor people and that his Beatitudes are statements challenging Christians to identify with the poor and the deprived, and to work to bring about a more just and equitable allocation of resources in society.

Jesus' Economic System
Jesus' revolutionary economics would turn the whole system upside down. The ingredients of the problems for people in many of our inner city areas have already been

described by Marx, and some reaction in terms of uprising and riot has actually happened in Marxist terms. Jesus had his own economic system: we have Christian solutions confronting us in the gospels, which are more revolutionary than Marx! 'Sell all you have and give to the poor', is just the start. The twenty-fifth chapter of Matthew specifies how Christians should act in Jesus' own economic community:

> 'For when I was hungry, you gave me food; when thirsty, you gave me drink; when I was a stranger, you took me into your home, when naked you clothed me; when I was ill, you came to my help, when in prison you visited me.' (Matt. 25:35-46)

These are prime obligations for all followers of Jesus and they make a mockery of many of our political, societal, commercial and ecclesiastical institutions which clearly do not obey these injunctions.

The criticisms against such a system are, of course, very reasonable.

1. 'If you go around providing everything for people, you take away their initiative and their ability to help themselves.' How true, but how wretched, especially when we are aware of so many people who have barely enough to live on, to wear or to eat, who are forced into a state of dependency, from which it is almost impossible to extricate themselves, by political and economic forces well beyond their control.

2. Jesus' economic policy was questioned right from the start:

> 'Master, you are an honest man, we know, and truckle to no one, whoever he may be; you teach in all honesty the way of life that God requires. Are we or are we not permitted to pay taxes to the Roman Emperor? Shall we pay or not?' (Mark 12:14)

If you had thought that to speak of Jesus' economic

policy was to overstate the case, it is worth drawing attention to this dispute. Even his opponents describe Jesus as 'teaching the way of life God requires' and notice the discrepancy between being a follower of Jesus and being loyal to the policies of the government of the day. I believe that this supports the suggestion that Jesus was teaching about his way of life in detailed and concrete terms.

His reply to the question is one of the most familiar and one of the most misunderstood texts in the Gospels. 'Jesus said, "Pay Caesar what is due to Caesar, and pay to God what is due to God." ' (Mark 12:17) 'But,' as one of my suburban church businessman friends asked, 'the problem is, where do you draw the line?'

Another reasonable question, but I'm afraid that it does not have a reasonable answer. It has a revolutionary answer. Jesus was careful to allow the worldly government its 'due'; but the reality for Christians is that *everything* is due to God! Jesus' reply is not about working out an apportionment, it is a confession of total obligation to God for all things as the one to whom all things are due—including concern and action for the poor and underprivileged.

3. The third criticism of such a literal living out of the gospel and its resulting involvement in confrontation and challenge, comes in the form of the question, 'What about reconciliation?'

It is worthwhile examining the word briefly. Apart from the reference in I Corinthians 7:11 which uses the same word as in Matthew 5:24 where it means 'making peace with', it is found only in St Paul's writings. It describes primarily a restoration of our relationship with God through the death of Christ, and it has a precise usage.

To transfer this concept to another context in order to argue that the deprived, the poor and the oppressed need to be reconciled with, say, the government is to miss the point entirely. Reconciliation in this sense means the bringing together of people or groups who have been separated by their differences. Now, a true reconciliation of this nature requires (a) that there was a conciliation or relationship in the first place, and (b) that the partners concerned are on an equal level and have an equal dignity in order to conciliate, or compromise, and come together once more. This is manifestly inappropriate to the relationship which exists between powerful, rich governments and businesses and poor, deprived, powerless people. This is why many people in the inner cities talk of social justice.

There is something still more exciting in the New Testament. For those who wish to follow Jesus and live his way of life there is a description of how the early disciples put it into action.

After their desolation at the death of Jesus, the disciples gain new inspiration and enthusiasm in their experience at Pentecost. Their first excitement was so overwhelming that onlookers thought they were drunk! (Acts 2:13).

Later on in that chapter comes a fascinating description of how those early Christians pooled their resources and began to bring about Jesus' Community:

'They met constantly to hear the apostles teach, and to share the common life, to break bread, and to pray. A sense of awe was everywhere, and many marvels and signs were brought about through the apostles. All whose faith had drawn them together held everything in common: they would sell their property and possessions and make a general distribution as the need of each required.' (Acts 2:42)

Here we have Jesus' economy in action. At the risk of being misunderstood, I would call it a kind of Christian communism. The nearest we have in our society to this sort of corporate sharing of life and resources is in the small co-operatives which have taken over modest industries like healthfoods. The trouble is that few people, even in the church, take this kind of revolutionary economic thinking seriously. I believe that it is what Jesus intended, not least because it is so revolutionary. It is hard for all of us to put into action thinking that will launch us into the unknown but this is precisely where our faith in Jesus' Way of Life, with his identification with and care for the poor, should take over.

3

Jesus Was Homeless

'Jesus said, "Foxes have their holes, the birds their roosts; but the Son of Man has nowhere to lay his head." ' (Matt. 8:20)

Don Cupitt, in *Who was Jesus?*, interestingly suggests that Jesus might have had a house in Capernaum where he entertained people, usually publicans and sinners. This house, Cupitt believes, was kept up until the family fortune ran out, and Jesus was forced on to the streets. Cupitt claims that there is clear evidence for this in Mark and Matthew and bases his claim mainly on the description of the call of Levi: 'When Jesus was at table in his house' . . . (Mark 2:15). It is impossible to tell from the context whether this refers to Levi's house or to Jesus' house. Matthew 9:10 says 'When Jesus was at table in *the* house'. . . making it sound much more as though he is in Matthew's (Levi's) house. The Greek is ambiguous and although it certainly seems that Jesus is presiding, it is far from clear that it is his own house. On the other hand Luke is quite clear that Levi's house was intended. 'Afterwards Levi held a big reception in his house for Jesus'. . . (Luke 5:20). It is worth following these quotations through because it shows the precise kind of detail New Testament scholars have to extricate in order to make the simplest point. It is also necessary to use common sense to complement the text in order to clarify difficulties, but sometimes it can lead to mistakes being made. In this example, although Don Cupitt's suggestion is credible by today's expectations of Jesus' behaviour, the text does not support his case.

As I understand it, we have no evidence that Jesus had a home after he left his family, and the saying at the start of this chapter seems to be a poignant vindication of that conclusion. Perhaps we have here a glimpse of Jesus as he realises the immensity of what he has taken on and the loneliness which must follow.

Jesus' revolutionary role was also prophetic. Prophets like Jeremiah and Hosea often lived out their own propecies. Jeremiah demonstrated that God would 'shatter this people and this city' by smashing an earthenware jar in public, and another time he wore 'the cords and bars of a yoke'. Hosea married a temple prostitute and gave his children symbolic names. Jesus demonstrated in the Temple, and made a symbolic entry into Jerusalem on a donkey. Jesus certainly spoke out on behalf of the poor and needs—which then, as now, could not have been guaranteed to make him popular—but more importantly he was prepared to act out his solidarity with them by living as they did. This meant that, being homeless, he was totally reliant on others for his needs including basic food and shelter.

The desolation of the 'foxes have their holes' saying also reminds me of the rejected Lear at the mercy of the elements on the heath, rejected by his family, just as Jesus was when 'they all forsook him and fled'. Does this mean that if we follow Jesus we can expect nothing better for ourselves?

This is a bleak view of life, similar to that which you find in the works of Samuel Beckett. *Endgame* is a ritual for two protagonists, both disabled, with aged parents like petulant children, but symbolically placed immovably in dustbins. They live in a grey world which offers no hope, but for the merest hint of a possibility that God might hear. Beckett developed this further in *Play*, in which three characters play out their eternal triangle roles trapped in urns and endlessly repeating their lines, forced into life by a point of light. If this is limbo then *How it is* is purgatory. It shows two beings travelling through a mire barely aware of anything but pain, only knowing that they must keep going. Nightmares, some people call these works, but they ring true for many people who despair of the conditions of their own lives. I'm thinking particularly of the single homeless, and the young. Those who, under the most recent legislation, cannot even board and lodge for more than a few weeks. There have already been suicides among the young who cannot stand such loneliness and insecurity.

To be homeless does not just mean that you have no shelter. It usually means that you have nowhere to belong, no one to care for you, no love and no support. It feels like rejection and it is a very difficult state to climb out of.

It is strange that so many tramps and vagrants are attracted to the inner city; I'll probably have at least one such caller each day. I usually ask them why they come for help to those who are already poor—I certainly don't earn enough to help everyone who comes to my door, but I can at least advise them of other possibilities. I also try to advise those who are already homeless or are about to become so. The fact is that much of the housing offered by inner city councils actually adds to people's problems in spite of a well-intentioned effort to provide homes for the homeless.

After the Second World War, eminent architects and planners got together to rebuild war-damaged London. Le Corbusier's vast space age ideas dominated. The plan was to raze much of London to the ground in order to rebuilt it in purpose-built estates running in strips from the Thames to the suburbs. Some of this redevelopment has been achieved, but it has not proved to be the success everyone hoped for. The faceless grey concrete blocks seem nearer to Beckett's purgatory than the space age dream they were based on.

One of the earliest groups who came to me for help in Brixton were a group of women who called themselves 'neurotics anonymous'. They all lived at the top of tall tower blocks and were scared when the blocks swayed in the wind. They felt shut in and cut off from their neighbours. The lifts were frequently out of order and it was hell to struggle up numerous flights of stairs lugging children and shopping. They were at their wits end trying to find a way for their kids to play safely outside without constant supervision. One of them actually flung herself to her death from her balcony. These are the bleak conditions of life for many of my parishioners.

Another difficult and protracted case involved a single parent—a father whose wife had walked out on him—and his three young children. They were trying to get rehoused from an old tenement flat with no proper bathroom, inadequate bedroom space, a leaking roof and problems with damp. They were put into bed and breakfast accommodation, which, although it cost a large amount on the rates, was in many ways worse than the place he'd just moved from—but he was assured that it was temporary. It was 'temporary' for more than two years while he still had to try to get work, look after his children and get them to and from school. Meanwhile the council offered him three properties all more or less identical to the property he'd had to move out of. After a lot of fuss, many letters and the involvement of an MP and a councillor or two, he was finally offered somewhere suitable. There was only one snag—it was full of squatters. It took nearly six months to get them out during which time this homeless family had their private hell prolonged.

Another old couple had their flat burnt out. They tried to live on in it, not telling anyone, because they had not been able to afford insurance. Premiums in Brixton are the highest in the country. We eventually found out through the local pub. They had lost everything and had no hope of replacing it even with help from their friends. Eventually they were rehoused but they still have precious little.

The plight of single people is impossible. When I got my first curate we asked the housing office to try to find somewhere for him in the parish as the council had acquired our old curate's house in the redevelopment. The first property we were offered was at Crystal Palace, several miles away, and the next was unfit for human habitation. The housing people had such a headache trying to find places for families that they found it hard to take a single person seriously. Eventually the problem was solved but my curate was homeless for at least three months.

A prison-like 'barrier block' has just been completed in Coldharbour Lane. It was built to protect the new Loughborough Park estate (which had to have all its ceilings taken out because of asbestos) from the noise of an overhead ringway motorway which was planned to run parallel with Coldharbour Lane. The motorway plans were scrapped in the sixties but the council went ahead and built the block which is not only an eyesore but which people did not wish to live in. It is now a refuge for squatters, single people and others difficult to house, but it remains a huge problem. The reason given for not changing the plans earlier was the cost, but the cost in terms of human suffering and damage to the community is beyond price.

Another notorious example of bad planning and housing leading to difficult living conditions, is situated next to my church. It is called the Angell Town Estate and was built to a plan known to create immense problems because of the experience of damage, vandalism and noise on the Stockwell Park Estate across Brixton Road. This estate was completed to a similar plan before even a brick of the Angell Town Estate was laid. The walls are thin and noise between flats is a perpetual annoyance. In three bedroom flats the smallest room can only contain a single bed if it is placed across either a door or a window. The communal walkways, which were meant to encourage neighbourliness, have become freeways and escape routes along which no one can walk without fear of challenge—this is the exact opposite to the garden path to a private front door! There are steps up and down to concealed front doors—a gift for burglars and a trial for old people—and the walkways are paved with rubber tiles no doubt to lessen the noise but in effect turning the whole place into a muggers' paradise. Young couples starting families cannot wait to get out and old people live in fear and trembling. The garages underneath are unsafe at night. No cars are ever left there and there are frequent fires. The new estates have won design prizes but they have caused more problems than they ever could have solved.

Suburban people will be familiar with the traditional village set-up which is still common outside city centres. They remain somewhat hierarchical, but they are at least on a human scale and the whole community benefits from the mixture of backgrounds and abilities brought together in a small population. These are the very things huge urban developments lack.

Another observation that I would like to make about the huge inner city estates is that few, if any, planners, architects or council officers actually live on these estates and have to suffer the effects of their own actions. The general lack of professionals in areas like Brixton also means constantly having to invite people in to service the area, like social workers, police and youth workers. As a result of these people not living on the spot there is no real sharing of responsibility for actions or any comeback.

I usually remind people that local councils are descended from Parish Church Councils and Vestry Meetings. The local churches delegated their responsibilities for looking after the poor and needy, providing clothing, and mending the roads to these bodies. These obligations were handed on in the last century, since when the old boroughs have been amalgamated. Local government officers no longer live in their own areas, they no longer mix daily with the people they are working for, and a whole sense of identity and responsibility is lost. Schumacher has taught us that 'Small is Beautiful' but it is a lesson we are all taking a long time to learn.

Christians could change this but it is hard work trying to get to grips with so many problems, being able to influence the planners, architects and council officers, and being prepared to lobby relevant government departments and MPs. Many of these people live in the outer parishes. I wonder how many suburban Christians, at home in their comfortable semis, would be prepared to take on all this extra work load? Yet we in the inner city, with all the rest of the problems we live with every day, are still expected to find the time and the energy to work to change the situation.

This is where Jesus' example puts all Christians on the spot—but it is difficult and costly to respond to this aspect of his revolution.

In 1982/3, the last date of a relevant survey, Lambeth's number of homeless households was, at 1,653 the highest in London. The number of dwellings declared unfit for human habitation was 15,340, the second highest in London.

'Jesus said, "When I was a stranger you gave me no home. . . I tell you this: anything you did not do for one of these, however humble, you did not do for me".' (Matt. 25:43&45)

There are now more homeless people in London than at any time since the war. There are at least three million people homeless in Britain today.

4

Jesus Was Unemployed

'On one of his teaching journeys round the villages he summoned the twelve and sent them out in pairs on a mission. He gave them authority over unclean spirits, and instructed them to take nothing for the journey beyond a stick: no bread, no pack, no money in their belts. They might wear sandals, but not a second coat. "When you are admitted to a house", he added, "stay there until you leave those parts. At any place where they will not receive you or listen to you, shake the dust off your feet as you leave, as a warning to them." So they set out and called publicly for repentance.' (Mark 6:7)

There are many arguments against taking the Gospels literally as they stand—and there are many difficulties about the accuracy of the sayings of Jesus which have come down to us. Indeed some scholars will accept only two, both of which are corroborated in St Paul's writings, with any certainty: Mark 10:11 (and parallels) on divorce and adultery and Mark 14:22 (and parallels), the words of the institution of the communion at the Last Supper—but even these have been disputed. It is·thus clear that an act of faith will be involved if we are to believe that an authentic picture of Jesus, his words and actions are preserved in the Gospels. When we make that act of faith, the Jesus we meet is staggeringly challenging and amazingly interesting and relevant. It is clear that many people were impressed by him in his lifetime: so much so that they tried to preserve all that he had said and done. This is made all the more impressive by the fact that he was executed as a criminal; which I am sure both the Roman and the Jewish authorities thought would put an end to the whole business. Two thousand years of Christianity have proved that this was not the case. The power of the Cross and Resurrection entitle us to trust that the Gospels do provide us with at least a very close insight into what Jesus wanted his followers to do and to believe. Much of this is confirmed by St Paul in his teaching which was written earlier than our gospels.

How far should we take our acceptance of Jesus' teaching and how far should it actually affect our behaviour?

Jesus' commission to the disciples is quite revolutionary. He tells them to throw all care to the wind and put themselves at the mercy of other people with almost nothing to protect them. If we did such a thing today, we would be accused of vagrancy. We may well be picked up by the police. We would be sure to be regarded with grave suspicion by everyone, and after we'd shaken the dust off our feet from all those who wouldn't have us, we'd probably die of starvation and exposure!

In our society it is almost impossible to live like that. You'd certainly get no DHSS payments if you tried it because you'd have no address. This brings me to the point where we have to admit that our middle class polite society, which is often described as Christian, has come a very long way from the kind of society Jesus envisaged.

Nevertheless in our inner city areas many people are forced to live more like those early disciples. This is certainly so when you consider the huge numbers of unemployed people found in those areas.

It is difficult to understand or appreciate the sheer disruption and pointlessness which large-scale unemployment cuases. Our young people lose their motivation early, while still at school, because they know that even if they get O and A-levels there is no guarantee of a job when they leave. Seventy-eight per cent of our young black people are unemployed in Brixton. And I am not talking about 'immigrants'. Most of these young people were born and bred in this country. This gives them an entirely hopeless outlook and leads to a population of alienated young people, who will grow into disturbed and alienated adults. They feel that society has let them down and has never given them a chance to show what they can do. It is not surprising if this gives them little respect for the society which not only is unable to help them but which seems to be actively rejecting them.

Unemployed people of all ages feel that they are unable to contribute in any positive way to the life of the community or to society in general. Furthermore society forces them to feel that they are a drain on resources. Just see how many editorials in the *Sun* and the *Mail* are constantly trying to impress upon those who live in our middle class suburbs that the huge numbers of unemployed people have only themselves to blame, they are 'spongers', 'living off the State', (although the State has declared that some levels of unemployment are inevitable), they are 'lazy', they 'can get work but won't do it' and that they are 'having life easy at our expense'.

Those of us who live in the inner city and who are parents, family and friends of unemployed people know how far that is from the truth.

One of my servers, Winston, belonged to a lively family who were mainstays of my congregation. Winston also had a gifted sister and a younger brother. Their father had returned to Jamaica and they had been brought up courageously and single-handedly by their mother, who was also a district nurse. Winston was interested in electrical installation and electronics. On leaving school he would have liked to work with his uncle in electrical installation as his trainee assistant. He had assisted his uncle in the past. The uncle was self-employed and, although he needed the help, couldn't raise the necessary money to pay Winston during his training.

Many people from the church and other friends then tried to help. First we tried to get him an apprenticeship. All the firms apologised, but, with all the cuts and economies they'd had to make along government guidelines, they could not afford to take on any new apprentices at all. We pointed out that this would have dire consequences for the future. They agreed but said there was nothing they could do about it as so many firms had gone to the wall already.

Next we tried all the various colleges offering courses in electrical installation, electronics or stage electrics. By now we had established our own drama project and were running a theatre company and could have given Winston plenty of experience ourselves, even by accommodating him in a sandwich course. It was all to no avail. One college secretary did confide in me that she was extremely sorry, especially as Winston's address was in Brixton, but they couldn't take any more on. A little more probing from me revealed that it was the Brixton address which was one of the main reasons why Winston could not get into courses. Another member of my congregation, Mark, also found that changing one's address did wonders for one's job prospects. One could argue that this was not discrimination, just being careful. One could argue that this was not racism, just a notorious address. Whichever way one takes it, it reveals unthinking prejudice especially against all the good and worthy people who live in Brixton. In the end it doesn't make any difference which argument you take, I can personally endorse that Winston's story is not exceptional. It is in fact a common story of frustration and dismay for many of our young people when they leave school and look for something to do.

Winston ended up making tea on a Youth Opportunities Project. His mother decided that she might as well take the children to Jamaica, although they were British. In desperation she said, 'They might as well be unemployed in the sun as here.' This, unfortunately is not the end of the story. The unemployment situation in Jamaica is even worse than here, owing to the usual post-colonial factors of a developing country with raw materials and little else. The family is now having to come back and face the same problems all over again.

It is not only young people who suffer from unemployment as the story of a middle class couple reveals. After many years of ordinary but fairly comfortable living, the husband became ill. He was then made redundant, but at fifty-four couldn't find another job. So the wife, who'd had a part time job in a hospital, went full time, in order to keep their eleven year old son and her husband, especially after his redundancy money had run out. She was taxed as a single person and, although she tried to claim for her two dependents, as a woman she was not permitted any more tax allowances. She then gave up her job since she would be £10 per week better off on social security—and yet she would have been more than happy to work on had she been treated fairly.

Since then, their small savings have gone; they never have a holiday, and can't afford any social life. Possessions like the colour television, the stereo, rings, watches and bits of jewellery, have all gone in order to keep up with increases in the cost of living. Bills are a constant nightmare as they are put up indiscriminately with little or no notice. Even paying off small amounts weekly never seems to clear the debt. They eat very cheaply and are depressed because they can't see any way of making further economies and they have no hope: 'Please ask Mrs Thatcher how she enjoys her coffee and cheese. We have forgotten what they taste like. Does she have half a pound of mince for her Sunday lunch? Does she count her slices of bread to see if they'll last a week? We have all been in bad health for the last two years. I'm sure it's with all the worry of trying to cope. My husband and I are both ex-service. Is this what we fought for?'

The indignity of the dole queue and the rudeness of many DHSS officers has to be experienced to be believed. I myself have experienced the helplessness, frustration and angers which results from trying to phone, write to or otherwise deal with DHSS and other benefit officers. They in their turn would say that there just aren't enough of them to deal with all the people and their problems, and that they need staff increases. Yet present government policy is for cut backs in this very area even though unemployment figures are known to be still on the increase, adding even more stress to the situation.

Living on £25 per week is not only difficult, it's impossible—as many pensioners know only too well. Government assumptions that young people can stay at home until their middle twenties simply increase and prolong the difficulties. To aggravate the situation, in my parish many of the families are unemployed in the first place, and one third of our families have only one parent.

The tensions and aggressions that result from having bored people hanging around indoors with no money and no aims leads to even more break-ups and trouble in families.

This apparent lack of compassion from those in authority who are, in the main, responsible for this state of affairs leads people to desperate measures, especially down the addictive escape routes. The pubs and betting shops become the main beneficiaries of the small amount of money given to the unemployed. At least they offer a friendly atmosphere and the possibility of forgetting your problems through alcohol, or of solving them by winning money. The increasing ease with which drugs are available inevitably leads to increased use, more terrible problems, addiction and death. But there are many ready to prey on the young and exploit this situation. Rich drugs barons have a vested interest in maintaining high unemployment levels in order to maintain their markets.

Another problem lies in the terminology of our economic theory. Our economic system sees 'labour' in impersonal terms, just another economic factor to be juggled along with capital, entrepreneurial ability and so on. But 'labour' is *people*. It should never be forgotten that when labour is described as a 'fluid resource', or considerations are being made about the 'mobility of labour', what is actually being discussed is how far people can be expected to tear up their roots, move house and lose friends and familiar environment—all of which totally destroy communities that have taken generations to build.

A society which is on the move, one that is homeless, rootless and without hope for the future, is incapable of respecting its surroundings and it cannot settle down. I believe that this is a major source of the anger which erupted in our inner cities in 1981 and 1985, when people felt acutely the undermining effects of everchanging populations who were merely passing through. This continues to have unsettling effects among local residents and in our congregations.

Trying to follow Jesus with no money and no resources, no jobs, no home and nowhere to settle down or belong is very difficult. But it is exactly how Jesus himself lived. Jesus, as we read at the beginning of the chapter, expects everyone to help those in this deprived situation, and we in the inner cities hope that other Christians may be able to help us. The kind of help necessary will only be of value if there are massive changes in the class and wage structures of our society. This has been amply illustrated by the massive pay rises which have recently been awarded to those at the top of our structures while teachers and nurses, and I may add, vicars, stay at the bottom of the pay scales. The *increase* in pay alone awarded to the Lord Chancellor (which he said he didn't want and wouldn't accept) was equivalent to the entire annual income of *four* nurses, junior teachers or vicars. I believe that we certainly need changes in pay structures and that Jesus would have demanded them, making it quite clear that nothing less than a revolution would be able to right the imbalances in our society where so few people hold so much wealth, and where the situation of the poor and the unemployed grows worse daily. Our present unemployment level is worse than in the Depression and it is still rising. We can only hope that it will not take a *war* to end *this* depression, because that could mean complete annihilation for the whole world.

Londoners bear the brunt of the problem in this country. There are more unemployed people living in London than in the whole of Scotland. Inner London has as many unemployed people as the whole of Wales. In November 1983, Islington has 2,550 unemployed residents per square mile; Hackney had 2,460, and Lambeth 2,200. It should be remembered that these figures refer only to those who claim unemployment benefit. The real figures are considerably higher. As we have shared in our clergy chapter meetings and our synods, a high suicide rate is linked with unemployment, a high incidence of mental illness of stress and depression. It is also clear that crime is associated with declining social and economic conditions, especially rising levels of unemployment. One probation officer remarked: 'Other things being equal, a magistrate will not pass a custodial sentence on someone whose job prospects are good or who is is a job already. If your are unemployed before you receive a custodial sentence, it is extremely unlikely that you will get a job after it.'

How can Christians respond to all this and, at the very least, try to follow Jesus?

In the first place there is little point in reacting as our present government has done by withdrawing money and resources from our inner city areas. This is the effect of 'rate-capping'. Christians need to be working, writing and arguing to get *more* resources made available for these needy areas. The Church needs to make sure that more able priests are encouraged to serve in these areas, even if their aim is to train the laity in building up strong ministries of their own. The dioceses must also make sure that those who work and minister and struggle to maintain a Christian presence in these areas are given adequate financial support, not only for their work but also for their private needs. At the moment the Church actually penalises those who work in the inner city. Their churches are not rich and cannot provide them with cars, equipment, secretarial help, a parish office, vicarage repairs and expenses the way suburban churches can. The small amount of expenses allowed by dioceses to inner city clergy are made as grace and favour payments instead of being a ready and welcome resource fund.

Christians have to decide whether they want people to spearhead work in difficult areas. If they do then they should enable those few who are willing and able to do such work in every way possible, giving them as many resources as they need. I believe that this is the point of Jesus' challenge. His disciples were commissioned to do a difficult job, but they were to expect every possible kind of help—whatever they needed—or they should shake the dust off their feet.

There has to be a revolution in middle class and suburban Christian thinking to enable this to take place today.

It should always be remembered that the Anglican Church is the established church. Christian members of the Anglican church therefore have a duty to confront their MPs and other members of government and local councils, (now doing their ancient church councils' work), with Jesus' revolutionary viewpoint. We should be prepared to argue and fight against policies that oppress people, victimise them, increase unemployment and make our people suffer in any way.

If we follow Jesus there must also be positive things we can do. We should be able to find alternative ways of dealing with the problems, and we should be prophetic. Somehow we have to see ways through this depressing present and unconscionable future. I also believe that it would be of great value if we could broaden our scope to include world Christianity, where there are many encouraging signs, and thus avoid the kind of constricting insularity which hems in the living gospel. Here are some ideas.

1. The Church of England has a great deal of wealth in capital terms, in land and buildings, in endowments and plate. Its investments are managed safely if a little unimaginatively, and some are tied up in legal tangles. If we want to free this wealth to put it to more practical and productive use, in the spirit of Jesus' commission to take no bread, no pack and no money, the main obstacle is the tie up between church and state. We may need to be liberated from the kind of historic security which is now clipping our wings. This may mean disestablishment or some other alternative. Something has to be done to enable the church to run its finances imaginatively and release its funds into our inner city areas.

2. It is possible to create some small jobs in a parish office although this alone will not be enough. There are many able people in our churches countrywide who should be able to come up with some better ideas. How about a think-tank approach? Calling church members in each church to have a brainstorming session together could be a useful way of pooling local resources. Some useful thinking could also be done at deanery and diocesan levels, but it must be practical not theoretical and may be daring. Putting our heads together could be creative and exciting. We may find some revolutionary solutions if we are brave enough to follow Jesus.

3. Another way to husband the Church's assets more

carefully could be by using them to create Christian communities. This has been tried before in terms of co-operatives in the exploration of socialist ideals. In the last century William Morris printed and designed his own fabrics and wallpapers, as popular now as ever. He made his own printing presses and printed his own books, poetry, chivalric romances and works of socialist theory. He is probably most famous for his involvement with the PreRaphaelite Brotherhood, who used many Biblical themes in painting and stained glass, but his Arts and Crafts movement still has disciples today. He proved that a human level of work and creativity is life enhancing and could lead to a revolutionary Christian lifestyle. Quaker families built garden cities like Bournville, to surround their work places with improved living conditions and a better environment for their workers. The Church could offer similar leads in order to give people greater security and improve their quality of life, as well as making their employment more constructive and fulfilling.

4. Christianity is a world religion and Christians should be able to offer some hopes and insights at a world level. A Christian initiative on solar cells, for example, could create jobs in this country, developing parts and technology for export to poorer countries to provide cheap solar power. Assembly in the developing country would create work until such time as the whole technology could be exported. While nuclear power is the dipstick which measures world power status, and the governments of the world continue to seek nuclear power to gain status, Christians need to prophesy against such a waste of resources. How much better it would be if Nigeria, for instance, could transfer from nuclear energy to solar energy which is free and abundant. In this way developing countries could save a great deal of money which could be used to improve the lives of their people, feed the hungry, clothe the naked, pay for education, and greatly improve their economies.

Such initiatives could confront big business concerns with Christian values, and encourage those involved to re-examine their own life values and profit motives. The shocking waste involved in EEC overproduction needs to be challenged in this way.

5. There is a need for some long-term thinking on the future of education, unemployment and retraining in the light of declining manufacturing industry and rising new technology. This will involve a revolution not only in our way of thinking but also in the structures of society as we know them. That society will change is inevitable. If Christians will take a lead in helping the world to develop through the present technological revolution in a way that ensures that people feel valued as human beings, the future could be liberating. It could offer us hope, instead of fears of redundancy and even greater unemployment.

Manufacturing industry is presently one of the greatest employers but it is likely that it will decrease in importance. The famous television advertisement featuring robots making cars untouched by human hand clearly shows the way. It is not difficult to see where this could lead, unless we take this imminent future seriously. We must help to build an alternative societal structure which takes these contingencies into account.

I believe that three main groups of industries will see most development in the future:

(a) The Leisure Industry:
Television, theatre, music, entertainment and the arts in general, together with all their ancillary industries including carpentry, electrics, electronics, tailoring, printing, painting, crafts, and so on.

(b) Education:
As 'leisure time' increases, so will the need for further training and retraining courses, as well as extra resources to cope with the increase in the sharing of knowledge and its communication. The Open University has shown the way, but all kinds of educational services will have to be further expanded.

(c) The Service Industries
There has already been an expansion in local government services and in Social Services. In direct contradiction with present government policies I believe

that these policies will need to expand further to accommodate the public's dependence on helping agencies, which will increase as the caring role that some firms once took towards their workers continues to decline. Catering, transport, hospitals and other service industries will always be needed.

The development of these industries, as manufacturing industry employs fewer and fewer people, will necessitate a shorter working week. So much so that I believe this will herald a revolution in our work theories. It will soon be pointless to talk about a thirty-five, thirty-two or even a thirty hour week when only three days will be necessary. I would like to suggest that in the future education could be expected to continue throughout a person's life, instead of being concentrated into eleven years between the ages of five and sixteen as at present. With the exception, that is, of those continuing to higher education. This would help cope with retraining and what might be called 'learning for leisure'. This would mean that we would work for three days a week and study for three days, *or* work six mornings and study six afternoons.

This scheme is likely to include some activities at present described as 'leisure activities' in an educational timetable. People could actually learn arts and crafts, cookery, food technology, dancing, acting, performance athletics and so on. This would be learning for leisure. The effect would be to broaden the scope of education in general so that it was no longer simply a vocationally orientated training ground for non-existent jobs. Education would expand a person's mind and abilities through the exploration and development of each person's special and God-given gifts. It would also allow people to try several expertises in a lifetime and retrain for each one. This revolution would also ensure that arts activities were never elitist, and would massively increase the scope of education in general.

Latterday Luddites in business and in unions are understandably frightened of such developments; but churches, understanding Jesus' revolutionary move to free us all, could help open their minds and change their habits, supporting people in overcoming their misgivings and fears, and enabling everyone to share in the bringing about of an exciting future and a general improvement in the quality of life.

5

Jesus Was Black

Try asking children what Jesus looked like and their answers will be interesting if not surprising. It's unlikely that they will have seen Pasolini's film about The Gospel of Saint Matthew and it's probable that they will not have heard or understood much about the Turin Shroud. But they will be heavily influenced by television, Victorian illustrations, Ladybird book pictures, paintings, windows in churches and the like. One of the most familiar images of Jesus is Holman Hunt's 'Light of the World' in St Paul's Cathedral. That not only shows a white Jesus, but he actually used a female model. It is a beautiful example of PreRaphaelite work, though not anything like as arresting as the same artist's 'Scapegoat', but all too often it is the only kind of image presented to our children. And children's corners in churches are still dominated by another familiar image of Jesus: flowing golden locks, blue eyes and multi-coloured children hanging on to each finger. Even our Brixton children are convinced that Jesus had long straight hair and a beard (probably blond but it could be dark since Robert Powell took the part of Jesus on TV), a long straight aquiline nose, blue eyes and long flowing white robes. If Jesus looked like one of the Israelis we are used to seeing on TV in newsreels about the Middle East, in inner London he would be called black.

This poses a crisis of identity for Christians living in our suburban and outer parishes—how could all-white communities cope with a black Jesus?

The answer is, of course, that they couldn't any more than black Christians could cope with a white Jesus. So many illustrated Bibles and children's books, stained glass windows and religious prints and paintings *prove* that we have created God in our own image, and he emerges as white. Hollywood's Biblical Epics, and recent television series have done nothing to change that image. The nearest I've ever seen to the truth was in Pasolini's film 'The Gospel According to St Matthew'—it does at least present Jesus with an arresting personality, a black beard, the appearance of someone from the Mediterranean area.

We are faced with a problem of identification. How can white people identify with a black Jesus? Traditional church teaching, as carried by missionaries to countries like Africa, India, and the West Indies, brought those nations a white God. Today we are realising that white Europe has no monopoly on Christianity. Indeed there are now more black Christians in the world than white. Their churches are growing and flourishing while atheists, existentialists and cynics add to our churches' decline. Other questions are just as real: how can a black person identify with a white Jesus? How can Chinese and far eastern people identify with either? We are lost in our own racism.

Jesus has the answer:

'He was still speaking to the crowd when His mother and brothers appeared; they stood outside wanting to speak to Him. Someone said, "Your mother and your brothers are here outside; they want to speak to you." Jesus turned to the man who brought the message, and said, "Who is my mother? Who are my brothers?" and pointing to the disciples He said, "Here are my mother and my brothers. Whoever does the will of my Heavenly Father is my brother, my sister, my mother." ' (Matt. 12:46)

The Christian answer to all aspects of racism is a firm and fervent belief in the brotherhood and sisterhood of all, whatever racial or physical characteristics we bear. This remains revolutionary in a world that keeps wanting to divide people according to race.

If Jesus' message is so clear why do many people remain racist? At the most obvious and familiar level racially offensive jokes still appear on television and in magazines, containing words like nignogs, coons and worse. Yet white people often ask, 'Why are they so sensitive? We're not being racist—I mean, what's wrong with golliwogs?'

The point is that if a racial minority—and Irish people suffer as much as black people, Asians and Chinese—is constantly being portrayed by a mocking image, its people worry that they will not be taken seriously. There are many white caricatures and jokes, but there are also many serious white images to counteract them. This is not the case for many racial minorities. Another question often asked by whites is, 'Why do they want their own black groups and clubs and so on—isn't this racism too?'

As a society we need to learn more about our common humanity, remembering that Jesus pointed out our common family relationship. Look at our own families. If one of your children goes mad on horses and another on computers, you don't normally force your horse-mad daughter to go to your son's computer club (or vice versa) because that is asking for trouble. They like to keep their interests separate and enjoy having their own circle of like-minded friends. It is necessary for black people and other minorities to get together to talk about their own things and share their common interests. It is bound to threaten those of us who belong to the white majority a little—we all share a natural curiosity to know what goes on behind closed doors. But as we develop our tolerance and awareness of other people, like a good family we will want our brothers and sisters to realise their full potential and develop in their own ways, exploring their own interests and specialising in areas that we won't all want to be involved in. This is just as true, for women and women's issues, gay groups and other minority interests.

Once we have begun to get to grips with all this; once we have begun to understand the extent of Jesus' revolutionary thinking and the extent to which he wishes us to change our hearts and minds and prejudices; we can begin to understand the excitement of those early Christians about belonging to a world family, and being a world citizen. We have so many differences, gifts and experiences to offer each other.

Nevertheless in our inner city parishes we have suffered much in racist terms. Many of our young people are discriminated against when it comes to getting jobs. In spite of many efforts to redress the balance in our educational system, black children still under-achieve even when high ability has been assessed. It takes a great deal of courage and self-confidence to escape the 'bottom of the heap' image so readily handed out to black people. When the 'sus' law was in operation we had many parents whose children had been picked up by the police for little or no reason. Thank God that this situation has now changed, but we must not forget that a substantially higher proportion of black people are arrested than the equivalent percentages of the population. This is not borne out by the conviction rate which is about the same. Accordingly there is too high a percentage of black people in our prisons, handicapped schools and mental hospitals.

To a certain extent this is reflected worldwide in that a disproportionate number of black and Asian nations are poor, and under-developed. Just a few countries hold most of the world's wealth while the majority of the world lives in poverty and starvation. As Christians we ought to be looking after those members of our family who are not being allowed to realise their full potential. In this country we already have an organisation with many Christians in it which is worldwide. If we took our own Commonwealth seriously we could develop it into one of the most exciting economic units the world has ever known. Present policies seem intent on destroying the Commonwealth. We no longer allow concessions to Commonwealth students. In this way we have lost an important role in world education, and our colleges and universities are the poorer for it. The USSR was very quick to fill the gap and now more Ghanaian students go to Moscow for Higher Education than anywhere else in the world. Small wonder if African States look to Russia for aid, even though the pay-off is considerable.

Our own immigration laws actually discriminate *against* members of the Commonwealth. There is no such thing as a Commonwealth family. Families are split up regularly even when proper marriages are proved to have taken place. Friends can only stay with friends for short periods unless they have lots of money. Members of our own Commonwealth cannot get work permits. I have asked many people how one can obtain work permits for friends who stay here from time to time, but it seems to be the best guarded secret in the universe. White South Africans manage to get British citizenship almost overnight. This all goes to show that our immigration laws are deliberately racist, proving to the world that racism is at the heart of our national life. Yet many of these same people have fought in wars for King, Queen and country and, until a few years ago, all held British Passports!

Those of us who live in the inner cities have much to be grateful for because, although we suffer many problems, we are also privileged to experience the kind of world Jesus envisaged at first hand. We know what it is like to live in a world family and we have experienced many of its delights and know its potential.

Take food for instance. It's amazing just how much you can learn about people by sharing their food and talking about it. In Brixton, as well as European food you can get food from all over the world—Jamaica, Guyana, Trinidad, Barbados, Mexico, Ghana, Nigeria, South Africa, India, Pakistan, Greece, Turkey, China, Japan and Israel. You can find out how to cook it all as well! Brixton market offers produce from all over the globe. You can't actually get best Lancashire cheese (you have to go to Lancashire for that) but you can get mangoes, pawpaw, breadfruit, chocho, dasheen, all kinds of yams, cassava, sweet potatoes, fruit, vegetables, grains, pulses and spices from almost everywhere in the world. The market is also a world meeting place. Friends of mine from places like Ghana and Jamaica have met people there they've not seen for years, and in the bread shops, the hairdressers, the tailor shops and the record shops you can make new friends in what amounts to almost an alternative way of life!

You also find out that cooking the world over is not so different. The famous West African soup is prepared by cooking meat and vegetables in water in exactly the same way as Lancashire cooks make their stews and hotpots! A main ingredient of one of Jamaica's national dishes is saltfish which is cooked with ackees. This is cod or ling preserved in salt. You can't catch such fish in the Caribbean—they were originally brought by British sailors. Another example of how cuisines mingle cultures. Guyanese and Trinidadian food is heavily influenced by their Chinese population in chow meins, and by their Indian population in rotis and curries. Jamaican rice and peas is also native to northern Ghana. Perhaps the time will come when we can enjoy a world Sunday dinner with all the family!

Another way in which we all share and benefit from each other's cultures is in music. This was brought home as never before by the massive Live Aid concert, which brought together the world's rock musicians to help the starving in Ethiopia. The way people have continued to rally to help this crisis has proved that racial barriers do not matter in the face of catastrophe. There is no person who can allow others to suffer starvation and die, no matter what their racial background, without trying to do something about it. This is ground for great encouragement—but it forces us to realise how much more we, as Christians, should be doing about it all.

We share musical riches such as were brought together for Live Aid in Brixton all the time. In this one inner city area you can find mediaeval music, jazz, all kinds of European music, Maltese, Chilean, Gambian, Ghanaian, Latin American, high life, Indian, Gospel, Soul, all the various West Indian folk forms: calypso, marengue, blues and, of course reggae.

This has been translated into the worship of our various churches so that even our more traditional worship is constantly being enriched by folk music, black gospel music, new classical compositions, Ghanaian songs, early English music and, perhaps most successful of all, a reggae mass and reggae hymns.

One of the most amazing events I ever took part in was an occasion which brought the whole community together. There was a local barman called Barnyard. I found out later that he had, in reality, a long and most distinguished name but he was always known as Barnyard. He was very active and noisy. He loved singing and was the life and soul of the party. Whenever I walked into the pub he would hold my hand and recite the whole of the twenty-third psalm before serving me or anyone else! He had been a preacher in his time and everybody liked him. Eventually he suffered a stroke. It was painful to see the spirit gone from this vivacious character and he must have felt it too. In a short time he had a second stroke and died. I was asked to take the funeral. We had about seven hundred people, I can't say *inside* my church because we can only seat four hundred, but they were all there standing on the font, on top of each other and falling out of the gallery. We should have relayed it outside. There were so many people I had to use the pulpit—something I never do normally. Everyone had his or her say, and there were a few tears. But this was a real 'send off'—it was a joyful occasion, a celebration of the life of a good friend of so many people in Brixton. Old cockney and south London families still turn out for a proper funeral but I'd never seen anything like this—and all just for a local barman! I felt proud of our community and I learnt much about how we can all relate, about friendship, about the values that, paradoxically, matter in life for all of us. That was what that man gave to us, even in his death. The rest of the story is local legend. We stopped almost all the traffic travelling south from London as we cut across to Lambeth's cemetery near Wimbledon. Friends told me that news broadcasts all that afternoon talked about traffic jams caused by a funeral! It was like something out of Joe Orton. There were two hearses: one just for flowers! And there must have been well over a hundred cars as well as two huge coaches. We had a police escort and we travelled through red traffic lights at high speed—one funeral car driver assured me that we hit sixty miles an hour, though that may be part of the legend. You couldn't see the grave for people. They all wanted to pour libations in, to give him a drink to see him through. After the prayers we all sang hymns and filled the grave—the last of the old Jamaican customs still remaining—while at the same time making a collection for the grave-diggers. People were still arriving long after it was all over. The Wake that evening stretched through three different pubs in Brixton. I don't believe anyone will ever forget that day.

It must have been something like that experience which so fired up the disciples on that first Pentecost day when people from all over the world seemed to understand them in their excitement. I believe that Jesus wants all Christians, of whatever race or nationality, to overcome those transient barriers and relate in a way that enables them to share that amazing spirit which celebrates and enhances life for all of us. This can be the kind of revolution Jesus wanted for everyone.

There have been other people who have tried to tread this path, some of them revolutionaries, and they have become martyrs. It is worth reading James Baldwin's *Going to meet the Man* to realise that, even now, in the USA the Ku Klux Klan hang people and burn them alive just because of their colour.

South Africa remains the most blatantly racist country in the world, which is why Zola Budd's instant citizenship was so resented. At last the world is beginning to recognise how many black people in that country, in their own country, don't even have a vote and are treated as sub-human. Desmond Tutu knows that he is treading the road of martyrdom; let us hope the rest of the world's Christians can help.

I have friends who have escaped the oppressive regime in South Africa, some of whom are black priests whose intellect and spirituality I greatly respect. They have escaped within an inch of their lives. They have been stripped naked, tortured and beaten for no good reason at all, except that they criticised their country's racist policies. Unless you have been to South Africa (it is worth reading E.R. Braithwaite's *Honourary White*) or heard some of the stories told by those who have escaped, it is very hard to believe. It is almost impossible to put yourself in the place of a black person who cannot earn anything like a decent wage, who cannot choose where to live, who will be separated from his own family sometimes by hundreds of miles, who cannot vote, who until recently could not love a white person (even if he wanted to), who may be taken away and put in prison for no apparent reason, with no-one knowing where or why, may be tortured or worse, and who is not counted as a person at all. 'I Write What I Like' was Steve Biko's proud boast, and you can read his impressive writings in a book of that title. But he was beaten to death for daring to do that, and even now, the doctors who gave false evidence on his physical condition are only beginning to admit the truth of how he died.

Martin Luther King had a highly informed vision of equality which he had the courage to act out: he was imprisoned and murdered for his pains.

We have these and many other examples before us. We have Jesus' own example plain and accessible to us all. It is up to us to change our thinking and our attitudes. I have been fortunate to meet such exemplary people in Brixton and listen to their stories first hand, but it doesn't take that for everyone to understand the earth-shattering truth that Christian love and friendship can break all barriers, and that Jesus wants us all to change society so that we may all benefit from sharing our different insights and experiences. Let us hope and pray that obscenities like the National Front will no longer be tolerated, especially as we remember that our fathers and grandfathers, brothers, sisters, mothers and grandmothers, uncles, aunts and friends died in the last war trying to rid the world of a similar National Racist Organisation.

The last word goes to Harry Belafonte, film star and black rights activist, who took part in the Live Aid concert. He was a personal friend of, and worked closely with, Martin Luther King:

'Eradicate racism and you will not eradicate poverty: eradicate poverty and you will eradicate racism.'

6

Jesus Was A Communicator

Introduction

When we look at the Church we have to admit that the medium all too often obscures the message. Jesus' challenging propositions have got lost in a clutter of tradition, sentimentality, and popular superstition. Jesus had to combat similar difficulties with Judaism in his own time. But it must be remembered that people in his time had different presuppositions from ourselves and different social mores. Miraculous stories of wonder and magic are no longer commonplace, not least because we have come to depend on ourselves to try to sort out the world's ills. Our society divides the sacred and the secular in a way that present day moslems do not, and in a way that would have been foreign to Jesus. Women have a much more equal and responsible position in our society than in Judaism, Islam, or traditional Christianity, though many people would like to see the sexes even more equal. The fact that Jesus communicates to us still, in spite of all this, is most remarkable. In trying to understand his message we have to be aware of three levels at which his teaching can be understood—the Jesus of his own time, the Jesus of Christian tradition, and the Jesus who communicates with us today. This needs to be borne in mind as we look at some different aspects of the Jesus we find in the gospels: Jesus the faith healer and exorcist, Jesus the teacher, and Jesus the demonstrator. Each of these aspects is communicated in a different way. Lastly I should like to examine how Jesus communicates to us in the city today by examining his interraction with the city in his own time.

First let us look at the communication process itself.

Jesus was a Communicator

Every year at the Carol Service for our church primary school we try to find a theme which will avoid the usual Christmas clichés. With the juniors, at least, we have been able to follow themes which will make them think a little: a pantomime about St Nicholas or a presentation involving Noah, the Ark and the Flood, themes which have a relevance concerning the significance of Jesus' birth but which avoid the familiar platitudes involving old curtains, teatowels and bits of tinsel. This year we had, paradoxically, a famine Harvest in order to send rice, flour, sugar and lentils to Ethiopia and the Sudan. Strangely enough this approach made more sense in the city than the traditional offerings of fruit and vegetables, even if the church didn't smell as good! Developing this theme we explored a Christmas story involving hunger and homelessness, trying to develop themes that are everyday life to city-dwellers. We learnt the Band Aid song 'Do they know it's Christmas?' hopefully showing how relevant Jesus' teachings still are to everyday life.

Some people felt that we were in danger of losing the magic of Christmas in the process. I fear that, all too often, the magic of Christmas with big red Father Christmases, invisible reindeer and spaceborne sleigh rides, is so artificial that it encourages our young people to dump God and Christianity as soon as they discover that Father Christmas doesn't exist!

The trouble is that our children know all there is to know about Christmas. Ask them—they'll have the answers ready to a fault:

It was very cold in Bethlehem, it was snowing. Joseph and Mary had to stay in a stable where there were an ox and an ass, who magically talked to each other at midnight. Baby Jesus was born in a manger (they don't usually know what a manger is, not yet having done any French) and was visited by shepherds (one had a little lamb) and by three wise men who were led by a moving star (Halley's Comet?—eat your heart out Patrick Moore) and their names were Melchior, Caspar and Balthazaar, and so on. It is quite pointless to explain that there was no stable, no ox, no ass—nor do we know how many astrologers there were, much less what their names were! It's no use giving them a Middle Eastern temperature chart or showing them the actual text of Luke and Matthew—they *know* exactly what happened, and all the Christmas carols, cards and decorations endorse it. Many things are communicated to our kids in ways over which we have no control. It is a pity that so much that is communicated is misleading and ultimately devalues Christianity.

We are told that the first stories about Jesus were communicated by word of mouth and oral tradition. A usual way to introduce this in Confirmation classes is by a game called chinese whispers, which can be hilarious and usually cheers the class up considerably. Arguably it accounts for discrepancies in our gospel narratives, as the message changes from person to person, but it can also be misleading.

Just as we know that some actors are dyslexic, so there are some world famous singers who cannot read music. How on earth do they cope? They do it mostly by relying on their ear and their memory. I remember when I was a choirboy of six, I could hear a tune or a part in an anthem and reproduce it pretty accurately—once heard never forgotten! But, as I began to learn how to read music that gift disappeared, until I could only sing the music when the notes were in front of me. One ability supplanted another.

It is true that at first much that we know about Jesus would have been learned and repeated carefully—and, once committed to memory, would not easily be dislodged. However it is easy to see how stories could be embellished in the retelling, rather like our popular version of Christmas. It is also reasonable to assume that different strands of stories or traditions would develop. In this way we can see how we come to have four Gospels all telling the story of Jesus, all different, and one, the fourth, with a background quite different from the other three. Certain traditions which came via St Paul weave in yet other strands. We also know that the Gospel writers selected and edited their material carefully, using their own gifts, whether it came to them through oral tradition or from written sources.

The process of communication was complicated and took at least thirty or forty years to consolidate into anything like the Gospels we know.

Nevertheless what clearly comes through is that Jesus himself was a challenging personality. He is shown as a preacher, a prophet, a healer, an exorcist, a miracle worker, a teacher, and many other things. He undoubtedly had enormous personality and charisma. He is often seen among crowds—and often trying to escape from them. But there are some aspects of the Gospel picture that would have been more acceptable in Jesus' own time than they are now.

1. Jesus the Faith Healer and Exorcist

Today we still have good preachers and some people who are recognised as prophets, if not quite in first century terms. Certainly Jesus' title of Rabbi or teacher can still be understood. However, faith-healing would cause some people to be a little sceptical while for others Jesus' exorcism and miracle-working would be a stumbling block. As it happens these things were also criticised in Jesus' own time.

> 'When his family heard of this they set out to take charge of him; for people were saying that he was out of his mind.' (Mark 3:21)
> 'They brought him a man who was possessed; he was blind and dumb; and Jesus cured him, restoring both speech and sight. The bystanders were all amazed, and the word went round: "Can this be the Son of David?" But when the Pharisees heard it they said, "It is only by Beelzebub prince of devils that this man drives the devils out." ' (Matt. 12:22)

Jesus reacts to all this with characteristic eloquence: 'How can Satan drive out Satan?' But how he reacted to his fame is not at all clear. If Jesus was a communicator in the modern sense, he may also have had the problems of many of our 'media people'. After some of his healings he seems to want to keep his work secret. 'Be sure you tell nobody', he says to the leper near Capernaum (Matt. 8:4); and to the blind man in Bethsaida: 'Do not tell anyone in the village' (Mark 8:26)—though how he could have concealed that he had his sight is difficult to understand!

Against this is the episode of the Gadarene swine, recorded in great detail in all three synoptic gospels. We know, because of the pigs, that this was a non-Jewish area, though the geographical details don't tie up with current maps. The significance of the story is found in the powerful image of the pigs, two thousand of them, rushing to drown themselves in the sea. This exorcism must have been some spectacle! We don't hear what happened to the herdsmen who, no doubt, lost their livelihood—all attention is fixed on 'the man who had been possessed' (or two men in Matthew) 'sitting there clothed and in his right mind'.

The people's reaction is not typical. First, 'they were afraid', and then (Mark 5:17) 'the spectators told them how the madman had been cured and what had happened to the pigs. Then they begged Jesus to leave the district.' This seems so strange after Jesus has just performed an amazing cure. Perhaps they were afraid for the rest of their pigs! And the last part of the story contrasts entirely with the secrecy about the healings so far:

'As he was stepping into the boat, the man who had been possessed begged to go with him. Jesus would not allow it, but said to him, "Go home to your own folk and tell them what the Lord in his mercy has done for you." The man went off and spread the news in the Ten Towns of all that Jesus had done for him; and they were amazed.' (Mark 5:18; Luke 8:38)

It would seem from this that Jesus is, on the one hand, a modest healer who is keen to keep his privacy, and, on the other hand, the successful exorcist who is publicly acclaimed as such. It is conceivable that Jesus was both, although the first three gospel writers all give us the story of Jesus being tempted in the wilderness. This is significant because, especially in Matthew and Luke, Jesus, in preparation for his ministry, specifically rejects magic tricks like changing stones into bread, political power over the kingdoms of the world, and spectacular miracles like throwing himself off the top of the temple and landing safely.

If these things really did go through Jesus' mind in preparation for his Galilean ministry—and he may well have described his wilderness experience to his disciples, though we are not actually told that he did—then it seems most unlikely that he would have welcomed the kind of public acclaim that attends many popular evangelists and faith healers today. What does seem clear is that Jesus saw his healings and exorcisms as signs heralding the start of his revolutionary new age, since giving sight to the blind and coming to the help of those who are ill were to be essential to his new community's lifestyle: 'If it is by the finger of God that I drive out devils, then be sure the Kingdom of God has already come upon you.' (Luke 11:20).

If Jesus the faith healer and miracle worker is difficult for us to accept at face value, at least we can appreciate the symbolism of such activities. It would be necessary for Jesus to drive out evil from the world in order to establish his new community. The physical demonstration of driving out devils showed that he meant business, much as the Old Testament prophets demonstrated their particular message. This is still real for us today.

2. Jesus the Teacher

Jesus' qualities as a teacher are universally recognised. In Brixton parlance he was a 'country bwoy', a provincial, and the better part of his life was spent in Galilee and its environs. This background undoubtedly influenced his teaching and is noticeable in his references to shepherds and sheep, sowers, seeds, vineyards and their cultivation, and other agricultural imagery. But Galilee was also a relatively prosperous trading area situated where major trade routes joined up, linking the Mediterranean coastal road with Damascus in the north and Jerusalem in the south down to Egypt. Merchants from Persia (Iran) and India would use the routes as much as the Greeks and Romans, and Galilee had its own produce like olive oil to export. This is the background for Jesus' parables about trading, investment, merchants, buying and selling,

land-owning, large vineyards, hired men and day-workers.
Friends of mine from Jamaica, Ghana and South Africa have
all identified the authenticity of the details in the parables
such as the men waiting for work in the market place.

'There was once a landowner who went out early to hire
labourers from his vineyard; and after agreeing to pay
them the usual day's wage he sent them off to work. Going
out three hours later he saw some more men standing idle
in the market place. "Go and join the others in the
vineyard," he said, "and I will pay you a fair wage"; so off
they went. At midday he went out again, and at three in the
afternoon, and made the same arrangement as before. An
hour before sunset he went out and found another group
standing there; so he said to them, "Why are you standing
about like this all day with nothing to do?" "Because no
one has hired us," they replied; so he told them, "Go and
join the others in the vineyard". . . .' (Matt. 20:1)

When this text came up as the gospel reading, members
of my congregation found it struck close to home.
Unemployed people looking for casual employment was
just like everyday life in Brixton!

This sort of communication through the ages is what has
helped to keep Christianity alive for two thousand years.
Matthew Arnold in his poem Dover Beach saw the sea, like
the sea of faith, as linking the ages in human experience:

'Sophocles long ago
Heard it on the Aegean, and it brought
Into his mind the turbid ebb and flow
Of human misery; we
Find also in the sound a thought,
Hearing it by this distant northern sea'

Jesus still speaks to us today, demanding that we bring
about social justice and help those less fortunate than
ourselves, through his example and his teaching.

3. Jesus the Demonstrator
The people who lived in the city, in Jerusalem, were much

more sophisticated than the northerners in Galilee, even mocking their regional accents. It was Peter's accent that gave him away after Jesus was arrested (Matt. 26:73). Similarly, today's Londoners believe that it's all flat hats and black puddings north of Watford! I come from Lancashire and the relationship between my home area and the capital city is not unlike that of Jesus' time. In Lancashire we still have old traditions, folk music and dancing, and superstitions revealing the last vestiges of agricultural fertility rites. There's even a long tradition, kept alive only partly tongue-in-cheek, of witches and witchcraft.

It seems reasonable to assume that this is why all the healing and miraculous work Jesus did belongs exclusively to this earlier period. Jesus was more readily accepted as a faith healer, an exorcist and a miracle worker in the credulous north than the hard-bitten mundanity of the city. Jesus himself seems to be aware this work is inappropriate for the city; as he says in a message to Herod Antipas:

'Listen: today and tomorrow I shall be casting out devils and working cures; on the third day I reach my goal. However, I must be on my way today and tomorrow and the next day, because it is unthinkable for a prophet to meet his death anywhere but in Jerusalem.' (Luke 13:32)

The word 'goal' is as ambiguous in Greek as it is in English signifying perhaps not only Jesus' destination but also his destiny, in his fatal fascination with the city.

Jesus laments over the city that destroyed the prophets and will destroy him. His words speak powerfully to those of us who do our best to minister in our cities today:

'O Jerusalem, Jerusalem, the city that murders prophets and stones the messengers sent to her! How often I have longed to gather your children, as a hen gathers her brood under her wings; but you would not let me.' (Luke 13:34)

Undoubtedly Jesus had a charismatic personality and

a considerable effect on the crowds who witnessed what he said and did. There are also some moments in his life when his personality dominates so much that he involves everyone present in what amount to demonstrations. Ellis Rivkin believes that these crowds may well have been enough to stir up the authorities against Jesus—especially since they regularly feared riot from the people—and that his very charisma may have been enough to bring about his death. The first demonstration is the call of the disciples at the start of his Galilean ministry. These men get involved with him with such little effort that it could only have been effected by Jesus' personal magnetism:

> 'Jesus was walking by the Sea of Galilee when he saw Simon and his brother Andrew on the lake at work with a casting-net; for they were fishermen. Jesus said to them, "Come with me, and I will make you fishers of men." And at once they left their nets and followed him.
>
> When he had gone a little further he saw James son of Zebedee and his brother John, who were in the boat overhauling their nets. He called them and, leaving their father Zebedee in a boat with the hired men, they went off to follow him.' (Mark 1:16)

This laconic account obviously has more to it than meets the eye. It is as if we are seeing the Jesus revolution in action at the very beginning, immediately after he has, as it were, issued his revolutionary manifesto. Catching people is what they will do to build up the new community.

The next demonstration comes at the start of his ministry in Jerusalem when the so-called 'triumphal entry' establishes his 'kingship'. Much of the demonstration is concerned with fulfilling Old Testament prophecy about the Messiah. E.P. Sanders suggests that if this all happened on the scale described in the gospels (Matt. 21:1-9; Mark 11:1-10; Luke 19:28-38; John 12:12-15) then it is highly likely that Jesus would have been arrested on the spot. The Romans did not tolerate upstart kings or alternative leaders. So much so that Sanders cannot see it happening just as the gospels recount it. His description is almost worthy of Monty Python:

'Perhaps the event took place but was a small occurrence which went unnoticed. Perhaps only a few disciples unostentatiously dropped their garments in front of the ass, while only a few quietly murmured "Hosanna".' (E.P. Sanders: *Jesus and Judaism*, p. 306)

Whether this demonstration was public or private it didn't exactly have the character of a CND march. However, it is linked with a third demonstration that has some aspects in common with demonstrations today—the overturning of the moneychangers tables in the Temple. This has often been interpreted in some vaguely 'spiritual' way as referring to cleansing the temple, rather like some Puritan act of iconoclasm, but the fact that Jesus could have acted in a down to earth and practical way should not be underestimated. C.H. Dodd suggests that it was rather like a manifesto in action. Taken with the Palm Sunday episode, other people have seen the signs of a political revolutionary build-up, starting with the secret password and sign which secured the ass for the entry into Jerusalem. Next Jesus takes command in the Temple, and one person even suggests that the Temple incident represents a planned attempt at an armed coup! (*Jesus and the Zealots*: Brandon).

I should like to put these actions of Jesus into a broader context. There is a group of sayings of Jesus which threaten the destruction of the Temple (Mark 13:1 and 14:57; Matt. 26:60; and John 2:18). On one occasion Jesus refers to the Temple and says, 'You see these great buildings? Not one stone will be left upon another; all will be thrown down' (Mark 13:2). (The words are almost identical in Matt. 24:1-3 and Luke 21:5-7). The reaction of the disciples is not to be scandalised, however. Quite the opposite; they ask Jesus 'When will all this happen? What will be the sign when the fulfilment of all this is at hand?' It is as if they were already familiar with this kind of comment from Jesus, especially when we realise that the Temple had only just been built and, in fact, work was still going on. Jesus' reply is not necessarily a direct answer to the question, and falls together so well as a passage on its own, with a style similar to the Book of Revelation, that it is often called the 'Little Apocalypse'. But it also contains one statement, found in identical words in Matthew, which ties all this in with what Jesus seems to have seen as his own mission and destiny in bringing in his new community: 'With these things the birth-pangs of the new age begin.' (Mark 13:8). If all this is linked with Jesus' actual demonstration in the Temple, which was a physical attack, then it seems clear to me that Jesus is acting out an attack on the old world order and hide-bound tradition that the Temple represented, much in the same way as he attacked the Pharisees. In the new age, in his revolutionary community, buildings and empty traditions are no longer important. Jesus thus changes the emphasis from external religious observances, found in contemporary Judaism and in Christianity today, in order to assert a belief in human relationships. Perhaps Jesus was demonstrating that the Church is not the building but the people.

The city did lead to Jesus' death, almost as if the city itself were a destructive force, and the Temple was destroyed by the Romans in AD 70. But out of all that destruction came new life; life which became Christianity.

Jesus' example as a healer, almost a travelling evangelist, is one with which we are still familiar. But this particular work of Jesus is very hard to emulate. So much so that he warned us about people setting themselves up in this way:

> 'Imposters will come claiming to be messiahs or prophets, and they will produce signs and wonders to mislead God's chosen, if such a thing were possible. But you be on your guard; I have forewarned you of it all. (Mark 13:22)

This rings all too true today when many people do set themselves up in all kinds of ways purporting to offer magical answers with false securities. In the city we are plagued with people wearing dog-collars who call themselves Reverends, bogus bishops bent on the extraction of money, and many curious sects like those which will allow their children to die rather than give them a blood transfusion or like Jim Jones's thousands who committed suicide in Guyana. The Jim Joneses of this world thrive on people's gullibility to such an extent it makes one almost grateful for the old Church of England which at least tries not to rip people off. City people, the deprived and the vulnerable, will try anything to get out of the unemployment and poverty trap, and are especially vulnerable to these dangers.

More familiarly, Jesus' teaching ministry remains one of the most important aspects of Christianity and could be further developed to provide a better preparation for living Jesus' way. We have a major resource in our church schools and much could still be done to encourage them to become better Christian training grounds instead of the vapid purveyors of a vague morality into which they have often degenerated.

We, in fact, need politicisation as Christians, which should go hand in hand with Christian education. We need to be proud of our faith and be prepared to demonstrate it just as Jesus did, and we need to communicate it personally. This will be costly and we will constantly leave ourselves open to criticism, and worse if we champion the cuase of the underprivileged. But so did Jesus and so have many Christians who have gone before us.

Jesus called the disciples individually and we also can often get through to people better through personal contact or personal counselling. But when we've taken them by the hand, and they have come with us, where do we go? Some might go to private prayer groups or house churches, but our main vehicle of communication remains our church services, and these rarely have anything much to do'with daily life. In these days of television, any theatrical, musical or 'live' performance has to be very sophisticated to gain credibility. Our Sunday morning efforts at worship rarely achieve those standards. Even what clergy wear in church manages to dehumanise them and set them apart. Our status games in the church seem to be based on military hierarchical systems with everyone struggling for his or her square foot of respect. It is a pity that levels of ministry were so soon demarcated in the early church:

'Within our community God has appointed, in the first

place apostles, in the second place prophets, thirdly teachers, then those who have gifts of healing, or ability to help others or power to guide them, or the gift of ecstatic utterance of various kinds . . .' (1 Cor. 12:28)

Jesus himself, as far as we know, had no such stratifications among his disciples and followers, but treated everybody equally, including the women, which was most unusual in his society as that time.

> 'You know that in the world the recognised rulers lord it over their subjects, and their great men make them feel the weight of authority. That is not the way with you; among you, whoever wants to be great must be your servant, and whoever wants to be first must be the willing slave of all.' (Mark 10:42)

This is a clear example of how in Jesus' own community, the usual values are turned completely upside down. Try telling Mrs Thatcher that she 'must be the willing slave of all'! Try telling any politicians, civil servants, or even church dignitaries that if they want to be great they must be our servants! Jesus' revolution was far-reaching and this is a salutary lesson for us and a reminder of how far the Christian church has developed away from Jesus' plans.

Jesus has communicated his message not only all over the world, but also across two thousand years. The message has often been misunderstood; sometimes it has been misread and it has also been wrongly interpreted. It is up to us as Christians to try to recapture the original content of Jesus' message and the spirit with which he delivered it. Only then can we understand and share in the excitement of those first hearers who tried to live out the teachings of Jesus in a practical and down-to-earth way.

> 'So much things to say right now, they got so much things to say.
> I never forget no way they crucified Jesus Christ,
> I never forget no way they sold Marcus Garvey for rice,
> I never forget no way they turned their back on Paul Bogle,
> So don't forget who you are and where you stand in the struggle . . .'
>
> Bob Marley

7

Jesus Was A Pacifist

Eighteen minutes past eight o'clock, on the morning of Monday the sixth of August 1945: Edith Sitwell began her *Three Poems of the Atomic Age* with a 'Dirge for the New Sunrise':

'Bound to my heart as Ixion to the wheel,
Nailed to my heart as the Thief upon the Cross,
I hang between our Christ and the gap where the
world was lost

And watch the phantom Sun in Famine Street
—the ghost of the heart of Man . . . red Cain
And the more murderous brain
Of Man, still redder Nero that conceived the death
Of his mother Earth, and tore
Her womb, to know the place where he was
conceived.

But no eyes grieved—
For none were left for tears:
They were blinded as the years
Since Christ was born, Mother or Murderer, you
have given or taken life—
Now all is one!'

The poem and the Atomic Age itself are older than I am. This makes it difficult for people of my generation, unless we have chosen to be involved in military matters, to understand the camp posturing and paraphernalia of war. It seems impossible to comprehend why anyone should want to dress up in uniform, walk in a stilted automated way and play with weapons which will cause death. The nearest I have come to it is in seeing the Remembrance Sunday service at the Cenotaph, or, going by Chelsea Barracks, watching men in berets and multi-coloured camouflaged clothing carrying guns, or taking the funeral of an Old Contemptible. The sacrifice of past soldiers who gave their lives for a cause they believed in we must all respect. It is just that that way of life is now, for most of us, forty years away. This is not so in Northern Ireland. War, guns, military fancy dress—even death and destruction—we see there regularly on television, but, because it is on television it has an air of unreality, of belonging to theatre and not to real life.

The real life I know in Brixton is part of the Atomic Age and it, like war, involves violence and suffering. Here are some brief character portraits, a handful of my parishioners and in no way exceptional. An everyday story of Brixton folk you might say.

1. A young man had an argument at the door as he was going into a party held in my street. Tempers ran high and a knife flashed. He managed to stagger to my doorstep— no-one helped him although he was bleeding heavily. He died in the ambulance on the way to hospital.

2. Another young man built up a thriving garage business. Slowly, with great enterprise and hard-won loans, he built up a good stock of the best equipment so that he could do top-of-the-league repairs and services. He was burgled. He managed to get most of the equipment replaced through his insurance and picked up the pieces. He was burgled again—but, on a technicality, his insurance didn't pay up this time. Six people were instantly out of work and back on the scrap heap.

3. A young woman had had six miscarriages. More than anything she wanted a child. She managed, through very careful nursing and day and night attention from her husband and friends, to keep her child on the seventh occasion. She had a beautiful baby which I took great

1. As a cage is full of birds so is our earth
   Full of cheats and frauds who set traps to catch other men.
   They grow rich and grand, drive justice from the land
   Crying peace where there is no peace
   Crying peace where there is no peace.

2. They profit from their power and ask for more
   From those who haven't got the money to pay
   They exploit the poor, drive outcasts from the door
   Crying peace where there is no peace.

3. Their prophets say, "It's never been so good";
   But the homeless throw their lies back in their face.
   They ignore the law and they sell the weapons of war,
   Crying peace where there is no peace.

4. The young have seen the lie and they show their hate;
   The old would care but for them it is too late
   With priests around to dress the people's wound
   Crying peace where there is no peace.

5. They have authority but they have no shame;
   They dare not change, for if they're moved they will break:
   In a crash to the ground their whimpers will be drowned
   Crying peace where there is no peace.

delight in baptizing. In order to make sure that nothing
was going wrong with her pregnancy she'd had all the tests
imaginable and it was later discovered that she had
multiple sclerosis.

4. A man borrowed money to buy a car in order to set
himself up in the minicab business. It took more cash than
he was expecting and he got seriously behind with his rates
payments and ended up in prison. While inside he tripped
down a staircase and fell on a warder. He was charged with
assaulting the warder and given tranquillising drugs. The
drugs affected his mind—he is now diagnosed as schizo-
phrenic and can't keep his life together, much less a job.

5. A couple got financial backing from their respective
families and bought the tenancy of a pub. The business
prospered, but the bookwork became a headache and, as
the profits rose, so did the brewery's rent requirements.
Being a multinational, its tenants are simply numbers,
publicans in the great British tradition are not even given
names. The husband turned to drink, the marriage broke
up, the business went down the drain and all concerned are
still heavily in debt.

6. Another young man was a singer, a performer. He
joined a forward-looking theatre group and eventually
played Ariel in The Tempest (Shakespeare). His performance was magnificent—he even helped to write the
music—he was a complete natural with bags of talent. He
got so stuck into his part that he read up background
material on magic, witchcraft and sorcery. He searched the
Bible and got completely carried away with the implications of the part. But, although he had an active and
creative intellect, his education had not given him the right
sort of tools to handle this information explosion. It tore
him apart, destroyed his family life and now he is
dependent on permanent psychiatric help.

The desperate tragedy of all this is that these are not
exceptional stories; they're typical of the frustration of
living in Brixton, a background to all the inner city

problems. Small wonder, then, if people react violently when, on top of all these catastrophes, people get shot, their homes broken into and all their belongings smashed up. When this is done by policemen it feels like a double violation because we look to the police for protection, not more violence. Such things do not excuse riots but they go a long way towards explaining why they happen; and that's even before any lids are lifted on drugs dealing, property rip-offs and protection rackets.

Jesus has much to say to this situation, because at the centre of Christianity, at its very heart, there is an act of violence. The Crucifixion itself is an act of violence which we venerate. Even more amazing is the continuation of violence done to people through the ages, like the *auto da fe*, the genocides in the Caribbean and in South America, and the Tudor executions and burnings in this country, all done in the name of Christ.

Perhaps this is best exemplified in our own times in South Africa where the Christian Dutch Reformed Church is a main advocate of apartheid, yet many blacks have found in Jesus and in theology a way forward for their people in spite of that inhuman regime. One of the guiding lights was Albert Luthuli, a Christian, a teacher, a Zulu chief, a politician and a 1960 Nobel Peace prizewinner. He found the Cross an inspiration in his people's struggle: 'It is inevitable that in working for freedom some individuals and some families must take the lead and suffer: the Road to Freedom is via the Cross.' Jesus' own words seem to speak for all who are still struggling in that country:

'How blest are you when men hate you, when they outlaw you and insult you, and ban your very name as infamous, because of the Son of Man. On that day be glad and dance for joy; for assuredly you have a rich reward in heaven; in just the same way did their fathers treat the prophets.' (Luke 6:22)

The traditional description of Jesus' message is 'Peace and Love' and so it is, but he also seems aware that the far-reaching effects of such a revolutionary message will challenge people in a disturbing way that at times provokes hate.

The core of Jesus' message is contained in Matthew's Sermon on the Mount and Luke's Sermon on the Plain. In this Jesus presents the case for pacifism before pacifism was even conceived:

'How blest are the peacemakers; God shall call them his sons.' (Matt. 5:9)

'You have learned that our forefathers were told, "Do not commit murder; anyone who commits murder must be brought to judgement." But what I tell you is this: Anyone who nurses anger against his brother must be brought to judgement.' (Matt. 5:21)

'You have learned that they were told, "Eye for eye, tooth for tooth." But what I tell you is this: Do not set yourself against the man who wrongs you. If someone slaps you on the right cheek, turn and offer him your left.' (Matt. 5:38)

'You have learned that they were told, "Love your neighbour, hate your enemy." But what I tell you is this: Love your enemies and pray for your persecutors; only so can you be children of your Heavenly Father, who makes his sun rise on the honest and the dishonest. If you love only those who love you, what reward can you expect? Surely the tax-gatherers do as much as that. And if you greet only your brothers, what is there extraordinary about that? Even the heathen do as much. There must be no limit to your goodness, as your Heavenly Father's goodness knows no bounds.' (Matt. 5:43)

It seems almost redundant to comment on these self-evident passages. But these same teachings have somehow been twisted to defend all kinds of oppression—not only South African racism but also the slave trade and even the notion of the so-called 'just war'.

Perhaps Jesus had the 'suffering servant' of Isaiah in mind when he was speaking of hitting someone on the cheek:

B. The True Cross

Michael Armitage

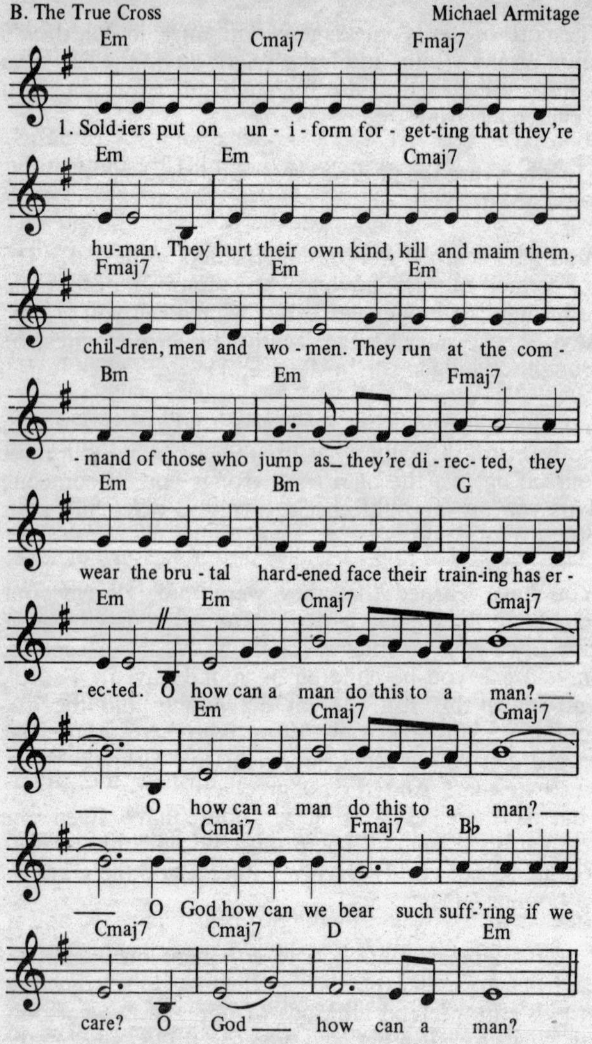

2. Frightened people peering through the grills of iron cages,
   Chained and starved they die, the victims of inhuman rages.
   We watch them suffer: pain rips through and tears the soul apart;
   And we are guilty — we deny our God a human heart: CHORUS

3. Bring back conscription, cat-of-nine-tails, thumbscrews and the rack;
   For those whom we hurt mustn't have a way to answer back.
   And how did Christ die? You remember, tortured on a Cross:
   Don't say that we don't have it now, we must make good the loss: CHORUS

'I offered my back to the lash, and my cheeks to those who plucked out my beard. I did not hide my face from spitting and insult.' (Isa. 50:6)

This seems so passive, which is uncharacteristic of Jesus, and could lead to the annihilation of all Christians in the hands of someone like Hitler. Ghandi has shown us ways in which passive resistance can be powerful, but in fact Jesus handles his outrage in a typically direct way. He screams at the Pharisees (in Mark) when he is confronted by their double values, and however people may try to explain away his demonstration in the Temple as 'righteous indignation', his symbolic act was forceful and almost certainly led to his own death by violence.

It is in the very context of the Cross and suffering that Jesus makes the statements which seem to contradict the Sermon on the Mount. Perhaps we are to see that Jesus lost patience with those who couldn't understand the message he was preaching, or perhaps his own confrontations had led him to realise that a message of love, peace and the redress of the wrongs done to the poor and needy cause violent reactions in those who have a vested interest in maintaining the status quo:

'You must not think that I have come to bring peace to the earth; I have not come to bring peace but a sword. I have come to set a man against his father, a daughter against her mother, a son's wife against her mother-in-law; and a man will find enemies under his own roof. No man is worthy of me who does not take up his cross and walk in my footsteps.' (Matt. 10:34)

In Brixton we are still struggling to bear our cross, and it often feels that we are more sinned against than sinning. Evidence of this came from the Scarman Report.

Lord Scarman took evidence for several weeks after the 1981 riots. He also moved around Brixton and talked to people at many different levels. He won a great deal of respect, and his report was welcomed as the fruit of that thorough-going and painstaking inquiry. If those findings and recommendations had been acted on by the government,

I am convinced that we would not have had any further riots. In other words, the 1985 riots were a product of inaction over Scarman's recommendations. This is a summary of his main points:

1. Racism
Scarman called this 'racial disadvantage and its nasty associate racial discrimination'. He was convinced that racism was a major factor in the unrest, but not in the sense that black and white people were fighting in Brixton as the right wing press insisted on reporting. He saw that black people are discriminated against simply on the grounds of their colour and that urgent action was needed against this social evil 'if it is not to become an endemic ineradicable disease threatening the very survival of our society'. He linked it with unemployment and declared that racial disadvantage and discrimination 'poison minds and attitudes: they are, and so long as they remain, will continue to be a potent factor of unrest'.

2. The Police
Scarman noted the long-term breakdown of relations involving lack of trust and suspicion from nearly everyone who lives in Brixton, whether they are white or black. Even local clergymen have been stopped and searched in the street or in their cars. This would provoke a major outcry if it happened in Eastbourne or Reigate: but because it is Brixton we are expected to accept it as normal. Surely this cannot be right. Far from making Brixton a 'no-go area' which is the last thing any of us would want, we are being treated as 'no-go' people!
Scarman's main suggestions included:

(a) Improving and intensifying 'community policing'. The bobby on the beat remains the best feature of our police force—but is not regarded highly within the force itself. Our local policeperson is called Pauline and she and her colleagues are well liked and respected in our community. It is the fast cars with extremely loud wailer sirens screaming out at all hours of night and day which unsettle and upset us in Brixton. It is also inexplicable behaviour like that which led to the shooting of Cherry Groce which needs to be examined much more carefully.

(b) Longer training would be one way to help prevent this kind of behaviour. Police training has been extended since 1981, but it is still only six to nine months. Compare that with six years for a priest!

(c) Police liaison committees. The old Watch committees preserved a measure of popular democracy but the new ones have not proved very effective. The Lambeth Committee is overlarge and includes a number of people who were appointed, not elected. This has led many of us to mistrust it in the main. However the Brixton Council of Churches elected our own member, Greta Brooks, who has brought her own saintly but firm qualities to liaison work. She has spearheaded the police station lay visiting scheme and, in her gentle but incisive way, kept us very much in touch with their work and the improvements they have effected in the conditions of those detained in police cells. This was a Scarman recommendation which has proved its value both for the community and for the police who are glad that their point of view is also being taken into account.

Hard policing methods remain controversial. In Brixton we are all anxious about the use of plastic bullets and CS gas—it can only make life less tolerable for all of us and force police into more confrontational and less human roles.

The other major problem in policing is to do with racism, as reports from America have also endorsed. If you walk into Brixton police station, for instance, you move from a mixed environment into an all-white enclave. It looks and feels totally different from the community which surrounds it. It also encourages an even worse 'us and them' attitude than the police normally find. But if the police are guilty at times of racial prejudice it must be remembered that so are the magistrates and the judiciary. I believe that judges should retire earlier—some are so out of touch that even with the best will in the world they are

C. With Love We'll Make Peace

Michael Armitage

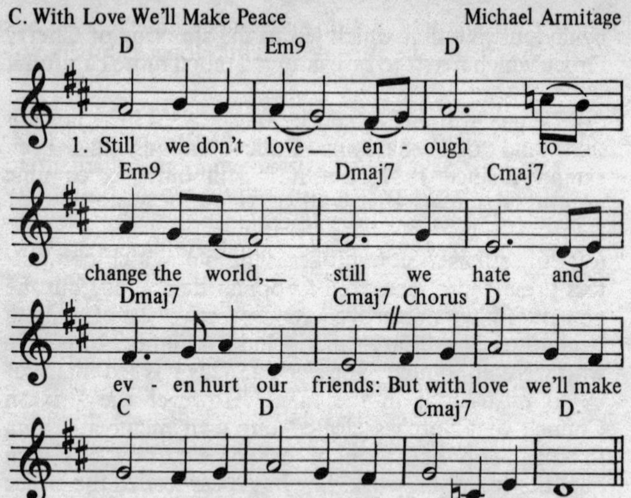

1. Still we don't love enough to change the world,
   Still we hate, and even hurt our friends,
   But with love we'll make peace
   And with love there will be no more war.

2. Still we have fears that we won't change the world,
   Still we dare not turn the other cheek,
   But with love we'll make peace
   And with love there will be no more war.

3. Still people die in order to change the world,
   Many fought before but still they die:
   But with love we'll make peace
   And with love there will be no more war.

4. Still we force people to kill to change the world;
   Making former sacrifice in vain:
   But with love we'll make peace
   And with love there will be no more war.

5. Still we don't learn that war won't change the world:
   War and hate only make more war and hate,
   But with love we'll make peace
   And with love there will be no more war.

6. Still we need Jesus' love to change the world;
   Love will break the barriers of hate,
   But with love we'll make peace
   And with love there will be no more war.

incapable of making a fair judgement. They also lack accountability and the appeals system is long, cumbersome and expensive.

3. Social Problems

Scarman said, 'The policing problem is not difficult to identify: it is that of policing in a multi-racial community in a deprived inner city area where unemployment, especially among young black people, is high and hopes are low. I identify the social problem as that of the difficulties, social and economic, which beset the ethnically diverse communities who live and work in our inner cities. These are difficulties for which the police bear no responsibility save as citizens like the rest of us.' He continues to give the context for the disturbances and places responsibility for improvements firmly in the lap of the government:

'The attack on racial disadvantage must be more direct than it has been. It must be co-ordinated by central government who, with the local authorities, must ensure that funds made available are directed to specific areas of racial disadvantage, particularly education and unemployment.'

He has been careful and considerate in his comments following the 1985 riots and believes that there is 'all still to play for'. Like us, he is more anxious about the effect of the proposed new offence of disorderly conduct which raises all the nightmares of 'sus':

'We must not revive in another form the "Sus" offence which, when stripped of its verbiage, ultimately reduces to doing something which a constable reasonably believes to be wrong.' Few policepersons would even want to shoulder such a far-reaching responsibility.

He has welcomed the creation of police consultative committees but believes that the police still have much to learn about search and arrest procedures and the restrained and disciplined use of firearms. As a Law Lord his view of the law remains equitable. He sees that the rule of law can only be achieved if it reflects social justice for everyone, including deprived and frustrated young black people: 'Peace will only come to the inner cities when the government provides social justice for all.'

The nature of these problems helps to explain what I believe is an important gap of credibility, experience and understanding between the haves and the have-nots in our society. In areas like Brixton where people are so vulnerable to attack from sources well beyond their control the priest is often the only person who can even communicate with the authorities in order to help. But the priest should not be seen just as a go-between—all too often we are saddled with being interpreters in order to stem the violence of confrontation between authorities and the people—but much more as a focus for all the pain and hurt, problems, feelings and sufferings involved. This is our unique ministry, and, like Jesus, it involves us with all kinds and conditions of people, many of whom we identify with.

In the inner cities we need more resources because we have the greater concentrations of people, and will use more resources. We also have the highest proportions of the poorest people who will suffer the first effects of any governmental measure. Many people in our inner cities also have a collective memory of wrongs done to them in the past. And many still have relatives living in countries which have suffered the violence of colonial exploitation. Brought up as British, they are now denied British citizenship.

Riots do not fit in with most people's ideas about pacifism, but the Anglican Pacifist Fellowship makes links between Christian pacifism and social action:

'We believe that the way of Christ is totally incompatible with war or any kind of armed violence. We are aware that this problem will not be solved merely by Christians adopting a negative attitude of simply refusing to fight or to kill; but we do believe that the Christian way of love offers a positive alternative to violence or war. The practical implications of living out this way of love are far from simple—as are the implications of adopting a Christian attitude to many other aspects of society and politics. If all Christians were to renounce war completely, the Church would need to face the immensely complicated social and political issues which would arise.'

How has the Church faced the issues of Christianity, peace, riot and all the related social and political issues?

The Church's reaction to what is going on in our inner cities has been mostly one of fear. Suburban churches have understandably reacted against public disorder much in the same way the Conservative government reacted; by wanting to withdraw even the support they were giving. I can understand that reaction—but if we in these areas are already hurting and crying out, what is the point of whipping us even more? 'If you prick us do we not bleed?' The withdrawal of resources—people, money and buildings—can only make the situation even worse. And, as a result, it's hardly surprising if we begin to feel that the Church in this country is a reactionary institution reflecting a reactionary government, with a deep-seated fear of the changes liberation brings. The church seems to care little for the message of Jesus which requires that we look after those in need.

There are times when oppressed people feel so strongly that they express their anger in unreasonable terms. Long term community suffering can result in community violence, even when that violence turns back on the community itself. Martin Luther King said: 'A riot is an expression of a people who have not been listened to'. Lesslie Newbigin sets riots in a nuclear context:

'The loss of confidence in the future is expressed eloquently in the mindless folly of the petty vandalism of those who can only express their rage by smashing up the symbols of meaningless affluence, and the equally mindless madness of the nuclear arms race between the super-powers.' (The Other Side of 1984)

The monstrous proportions of nuclear power has led to world fear in the realisation that our future rests in too few hands. This has encouraged a renewal of interest in CND and various anti-nuclear lobbies like Lawyers for Nuclear Disarmament. Here are three of the latter's interim findings from their London Nuclear Warfare Tribunal:

(a) It is now established beyond reasonable doubt that

any major nuclear exchange would be an unprecedented human and environmental catastrophe, posing a serious threat to the survival of all life on the planet. One aspect of this threat has been dramatised by the experimental findings that soot and dust from nuclear explosions totalling no more than one hundred megatons could produce a 'nuclear winter' of at least several months duration.

(b) The evidence was overwhelmingly convincing that there is no acceptable way to reconcile these weapons, developments and strategies with prevailing morality, either as interpreted by the main world religions or by the leading ideas of non-religious political ethics.

(c) The evidence established that resources devoted to war are excessive and wasteful, even given a commitment to military methods of self-defence, and that this circumstance greatly complicates the challenge of overcoming widespread poverty at home and abroad, an effect especially shocking at this time of massive famine in sub-Saharan Africa.'

One of the main problems is that nuclear power has become the dipstick which measures world power status, and the various governments in the world continue to seek nuclear power to gain status. It seems lunatic for oil-rich and sunny Nigeria to use its resources on nuclear power when it could exploit solar power infinitely more cheaply. Even European industrialists could surely see that the export of their own technology on a modest scale could aid struggling African nations.

But vested interests in the 'defence' business cannot allow such development. The political game gets very complicated: some economies rely on arms and 'defence vehicles' manufacture for their solvency, and inevitably education and public services suffer in favour of defence spending. It has even been argued that high unemployment is necessary to persuade people to serve in the armed forces. I believe that Christians cannot proclaim forcefully enough that when people undergo military training, whatever else they may learn, they are being trained to kill other people.

The current defence budget in the United Kingdom costs each working person £15 per week. Should Christians allow their money to be spent in this way?

Defence spending in this country has been estimated at £700 per person per year—more than spending on education, health and housing put together. The world spends £24 billion a fortnight on defence and armaments—more than enough to provide food, water, education, health and housing for everyone in the world for a whole year!

In the community that Jesus envisaged we have to overcome all such hurt and waste, with so many resources put towards destruction. Any system which creates a situation where people feel powerless and oppressed, violated and hopeless, helpless, less than human, is itself violent. The way to making peace is found in a sustained and wholehearted commitment to change, on such a scale that it would transform our society into a caring one whose primary concern would be the eradication of the sufferings of disadvantaged people.

The way of Jesus is not the way of the plastic bullet, the gun, the bludgeon, or the petrol bomb. Nor is it the way of high unemployment, bad housing, social deprivation or self-seeking criminality. Nor is the way of Jesus a way of waiting for the next general election, the next millenium or, God forbid, the next war.

The time for Jesus' revolution is now.

'True peace is not merely the absence of tension; it is the presence of justice.'

'The church cannot be silent while mankind faces the threat of nuclear annihilation. If the church is true to her mission, she must call for an end to the arms race.'

Martin Luther King

8

Jesus Criticised Authority

Matthew 23:13: Alas, alas for you lawyers and Pharisees, hypocrites that you are! You shut the door of the Kingdom of Heaven in men's faces; you do not enter yourselves, and when others are entering, you stop them.

14: Alas for you, lawyers and Pharisees, hypocrites! You eat up the property of widows, while you say long prayers for appearance' sake. You will receive the severest sentence.

15: Alas for you, lawyers and Phraisees, hypocrites! You travel over sea and land to win one convert, and when you have won him you make him twice as fit for hell as yourselves.

16: Alas for you, blind guides! . . . Blind fools! . . .

24: Blind guides! You strain off a midge, yet gulp down a camel . . .

33: You snakes, you vipers' brood, how can you escape being condemned to hell?

(compare Luke 11:39-52)

Jesus has disputes with and heavily criticises those in authority in all four gospels. This section is staggering because of the violence of the language—not at all the typical church view of 'gentle Jesus meek and mild'! I don't know how any of us would react to being called 'snakes' or 'vipers' brood', but it was clearly a considerable insult to the Pharisees and lawyers, snakes and vipers being identified with evil (Genesis 3).

The scholars tell us that in first century Judaism this kind of outburst would have caricatured the Pharisees and lawyers. Even so it seems to me that Jesus' pronouncements and outbursts, as we have them in Matthew, are very apt and expressive warnings to all people who are in positions of authority, especially in the church, the legal profession, and the government. His words certainly remain a powerful warning to all Christians against double dealing, double values and hypocrisy.

In the inner city this is especially significant because, since our areas act as a focus for so many of the worst aspects of our society, people who live there come into contact with more authority figures more often than in other areas. There is also a feeling that authorities are antagonistic to inner city communities rather than compassionate.

The Police
This is especially true of the police. Much has been written and said about their changing role in our society and now, as John Alderson describes, they are increasingly being used as a front-line arm of the government. This takes them away from their traditional role as guardians of law and order with the general consent of the electorate and the community. This has been self-evident in the way in which the police have dealt with the conflicts and riots in Brixton since 1981.

At the local level the last few years have marked a change in policy along the lines Lord Scarman suggested in his report. The most important aspect of which has been some effort to restore neighbourhood policing, in recognition of the fact that the bobby on the beat has been, and hopefully will continue to be, an important link-person in the chain of authority. This is not to deny that more needs to be done to restore friendly community relations free of suspicion on either side.

One thing I am convinced of is that the kinds of 'Neighbourhood Watch' schemes which often work well in outer and suburban areas are not appropriate forms of community policing for many areas in the inner city where there is a changing population. Even next door neighbours in places like Brixton do not know each other, which means such schemes could lead to suspicion of snooping and encroaching on privacy.

The police/community liaison committees have not been successful either, largely because when they were set up their membership was chosen by the police and the Home Office. Although representatives from other bodies like the local Council of Churches were eventually invited on, suspicion remains and can only be countered by making membership a totally democratic process with elected members from community groups.

On the other hand, one good move has been the formation of a team of prison visitors, actively supported by the Brixton Council of Churches, and again stemming from one of Scarman's recommendations. Although there is a long way to go, I believe that some good things have happened which have done much to lessen suspicion on both sides; though the scheme has pointed out specific problems like the primitive conditions in local police cells and the difficulties surrounding people's rights on arrest. These seem to be far from clear and leave people unnecessarily confused.

The most significant change was made, however, when Commander Marnoch took over locally. For the first time he admitted that the police could make mistakes. This defused the situation for many people and brought things back to a human and humane level. It always helps to know that those in authority are human too!

Another important aspect of having authority is that the people with power should know the people they have authority over. Few people with power over others have long experience of living in inner city areas, some have none at all. I believe that it would be of great value if those policemen who are to come and work in inner city areas were able first to experience what it is like in these areas, in their training. I would suggest that several months spent on placements in youth centres or with other community groups in inner city areas would be of great value in police training. This has been shown to work in one of our Lambeth Youth Clubs which has flourished under the leadership of a local black youth leader and a local policeman. Their personalities, their close involvement and their team work have helped to allay a great deal of mistrust, especially among young black people.

Incidentally I also think that some months in an inner city parish should be included in the training of all priests, fewer and fewer of whom are concerned about inner city ministry, and similar placements in other helping professions.

Various Authorities
I have already touched on housing, planning and local government and the difficulties of trying to solve problems which those in authority do not experience themselves. The problems of single and lonely people of all age groups are remarkably similar throughout this country but there are strong forces outside an individual's control which vary as considerably as each person's ability to cope varies. The most startling difference I have found between ministering to people in an outer parish and in an inner city area has been in the amount of involvement needed with major institutions, local councils and governmental departments for day to day life in inner areas. Trying to help people in the inner city means constantly running up against various authorities. Take court cases and legal procedure, for instance—not that I know much about it! The simple truth is that I can cope with it all much better than many of my parishioners who soon become overwhelmed by impersonal language and formal procedures.

It is the same story with DHSS Officers, in their offices and on the phone—trying to claim people's rightful money and finding them places to live; with housing officers of the local council over repairs, damp problems, security, moves and flat changes; with social workers and their clients, some of whom would deal with me but would not allow any 'outside interference'—in one case I even had to help restore a child to a family after she had been put into 'permanent fostering' by mistake—people with nowhere to live, people just out of prison; and all kinds of people who are frustrated and demoralised by unemployment.

I was personally involved, with my church, in six months of dispute with the local authority, trying to persuade the council that it ought not to close down all the approach roads to my church! This was only achieved by a massive effort from the whole of the local community in a formal Public Inquiry.

Another shockingly time-consuming place to while away the hours is the Home Office Immigration Department in Lunar House, Croydon. It has taken up to two days—'please come back tomorrow'—after hours of waiting, simply to get visas extended for members of our own Commonwealth. Our present immigration laws run precisely against Jesus' teaching: he said, 'When I was a stranger you took me into your home.' It is hard to know just what to do when you have seen the pain in people's faces on TV newsreels as the wife or husband of a valid married couple is deported because the immigration authorities believe they intend to settle here. So what? Every year there are more people leaving this country than coming to settle here—something the right wing press don't tell us as they try to suggest that immigration is overwhelming. Things have become so insensitive that if an English husband or wife dies, the other partner is sometimes deported with unseemly haste, and to hell with what happens to the children! Relationships across international borders cannot exist unless there is a blood tie or £150,000. This is inhuman and intolerable to those who follow Jesus.

Jesus' instruction, 'When I was in prison you visited me', has led me into almost every prison in the country. It has made me acutely aware of how much reform our prison system needs. Those on remand—i.e. innocent by British law—have fewer rights and fewer privileges than those committed on an offence. Realising this I once made an effort, enlisting the help of Community Service Volunteers, to try to get people to teach remand prisoners in Pentonville Prison to read and write, as well as

offering other cultural classes. This suggestion met with a
firm refusal, mainly because of anxieties about
supervision, even though it would have cost the
authorities nothing.

Our prisons are a disgrace even if one supports the
punitive theory on which they are based. The fact that
cells have no toilets means that prisoners have to carry
their full pails each morning to a sink to empty them.
This degradation is not found in other European prisons.

There is immense scope for reform, not to mention
revolution, in our prison system, and Jesus was specific
about the involvement of his followers in this. It ought to
be a crusade for all Christians: maybe then the authorities
would listen.

The fact that all these occasions of coming up against
authority are more or less everyday experiences in the
inner city should help to explain why there should be a
credibility gap between city-dwellers and those outside. It
is almost impossible for the majority of people in this
country, the ordinary white middle class people, to
experience or understand exactly what it is like to live in
an environment in which the problems pile up so quickly
and so regularly, and in which almost every area of life
seems vulnerable to the imposition of power from sources
beyond most people's control.

Often the priest is one of the few, if not the only
person, living on the spot who can even communicate
with the relevant authorities in order to help. This has
somehow to be shared with other Christians and could
certainly involve those who live in the stronger outer
parishes if they would be prepared to take on such
responsibility.

Government

Even though many inner city areas have made themselves
heard, even though through riots this country has been
sensitised to the needs of those who live in places like
Brixton, Toxteth, Birmingham, Manchester and Leeds,
even though people in those areas have tried to help
themselves with small job creation schemes and educational projects, unemployment rises, living conditions

worsen, local communities have their grants cut back even further and there seems to be little or no response from those in authority in the government.

It is now a truism to say that massive amounts of money and resources need to be poured into the inner cities, but it has not yet happened.

Politics and economics are forces which affect us all but the inner cities feel the pinch first, since they have greater concentrations of the poorest people. The present government's economic policies have in fact made life in the inner city increasingly painful with cuts in expenditure on education, health, local amenities, housing and community projects. This has stifled a great deal of local initiative, and yet nothing has been done to lessen the numbers of unemployed people who increasingly need all these facilities. It seems, sometimes, as if people in the inner cities are sacrificial offerings to a merciless economic god.

This is a scandal which should attract outrage and concern from all who believe in Jesus' way of life since it reveals a considerable disregard for the poor, the needy and the oppressed by those in authority. But in case there should be any genuine misunderstanding, Christians should waste no time in sensitising those in authority to genuine human misery and suffering at all levels, whether it is caused by cuts to inner city projects or by cuts in aid to developing countries. The injustices of the increasing gap between the rich and the poor in this country and in the world should constantly be pressed on the government, whichever party is in power, as well as the obscenity of the EEC's overproduction and waste of foodstuffs. It would be worthwhile to organise a Christian conscience to question those in authority in the EEC about their policies which create artificially high price levels and immoral stockpiles of food. Bob Geldof spoke for many ordinary people when he challenged those in authority in Brussels about their indecent and immoral stockpiling of foodstuffs, and declared that they needed a laxative! He spoke for many of us who do not have access to those authorities and yet feel acutely the injustices involved in current EEC policies. Jesus wanted us to feed the hungry and we should be able to share our food resources with other countries to save people starving to death. The cost of transporting surplus food is actually lower than the cost of storing the grain, butter, beef and the rest of the mountains. Financial aid has to be backed up with the expertise of people, technology and teachers. British aid for developing countries has actually fallen by 18% since 1980.

Christians must continue to help those in authority to understand the challenge of Jesus' teaching so as to influence their judgement and encourage their action in caring for all the world's people.

Individual action is rarely enough to convince those in authority. As Bishop David Sheppard has pointed out, some changes can only be made through the ballot box and by raising the most important issues at election time. The trouble is that Jesus' system is revolutionary. If we truly share all our resources with those in need, we shall be left the poorer. I wonder how many of us are actually prepared to take a cut in our standard of living, so that people in Ethiopia and the Sudan can live.

The Church

Looking at his words in Matthew's Gospel, I wonder what Jesus would say about the Church and its structures today. Would he say, 'Well done thou good and faithful servants', or would he say, 'Get from my sight to the eternal fire'. . .? He would certainly be critical.

Even in Victorian times, the church established education for the poor, worked against slavery, improved working conditions, especially for children—Charles Kingsley's *The Water Babies* made a great impact, though Mayhew's and Dickens' works were more important—transformed hospital conditions and even tried to reform prisons. Except in the area of youth work the church has done little of any significance to improve the lot of the poor and needy in this country in this century, especially since the war. Sometimes the church's middle class image gets in the way of living out the gospel.

At a grassroots level it is hard for ordinary church people to deal with any authorities and church authorities are no exception. Committee procedures and synodical government actually prevent ordinary Christian people's voices from being heard. Our processions of dignitaries and parades of finery, though undoubtedly impressive, often seem amazingly close to the very things Jesus criticised:

> 'Beware of the doctors of the law, who love to walk up and down in long robes, receiving respectful greetings in the street, and to have the chief seats in synagogues, and places of honour at feasts.' (Mark 12:38)

How familiar all this still seems—how little have Jesus' warnings been heeded. I believe that Jesus' way was to turn values upside down, which is why I choose to call his system revolutionary. Jesus actually saw those in authority as the servants of us all; not as those who always know better and sometimes believe they have to teach us a lesson!

> 'You know that in the world the recognised rulers lord it over their subjects, and their great men make them feel the weight of authority. That is not the way with you; among you, whoever wants to be great must be your servant, and whoever wants to be first must be the willing slave of all. For even the Son of Man did not come to be served but to serve.' (Mark 10:42)

In John's Gospel, Jesus himself acts this out when he washes the disciples' feet like a servant. Peter objects to such abasement but is carefully put in his place: 'If I, your Lord and Master, have washed your feet, you ought also to wash one another's feet. I have set an example: you are to do as I have done for you.'

How much we, as Christians, still have to learn from such revolutionary behaviour.

In Brixton we became so concerned that the church's middle class structures were actually inhibiting many of our able ordinary working-class church people from using their gifts that we tried to separate from those nearby parishes which were dominated by the white middle classes.

We were joined with them by an accident of history and decided to try to go it alone. They were hurt by this move, though exactly why was not at all clear, and could not understand why it was so important for the Brixton churches to compare notes and pool their own resources. The 'Brixton Experiment', as it has been called, has been valuably informative about how structures work or, indeed, don't work. At the start there was much pressure to form a committee, but this was resisted until we were sure that the committee model was the right one for us. The result is something of a compromise—two chair-persons, a two-person secretariat and a treasurer. However all meetings remain open to all Brixton church people and there is a space in every meeting for each person present to speak if they so wish. The result is that our lay people have actually been enjoying meetings that were previously a boring chore. We have been sharing issues which really affect us all and it is noticeable that the clergy are not always in the forefront—in fact we are learning a great deal by actually being allowed to serve instead of being always expected to lead. It is early days yet, but it has already given our church people in Brixton an added confidence to know they are sharing problems at a human level rather than playing procedural games. All of which is most encouraging if not exactly revolutionary!

Nevertheless church structures do need to be shaken and many need to justify their existence. If, for instance, we cannot afford more clergy working with the people in the inner city, can we afford bishops? Do we really need them, are they really serving us, or would trained lay administrators be more helpful and efficient? The synodical system is cumbersome and non-represent-ative—there was only one young black person in the last Southwark Diocesan Synod and he came from my parish!—and it fails to communicate with or be relevant to ordinary people. Yet it is these people who put the money in the collection plate and it is precisely with these people that Jesus seemed to communicate best. How can the church champion the cause of the unemployed if (a) it does not represent them in its own structures, and (b) it does not communicate in a lively way they can understand?

The distribution of the church's wealth needs careful reappraisal and money put where it is most needed. If the government is not giving enough help to the poor, the needy and the unemployed, then Christians need to pressurise the church to set up its own schemes with centralised funding.

Ministry in new shapes and forms needs to be recognised where it is happening. A way should be made for the recognition of the ministries of non-academic working-class people, who should not be forced to cope with middle class obstacle races in order to be ordained, but encouraged to explore and develop their own great gifts. This is what Jesus did with his own disciples. Brixton's Anglican clergy have tried to be specific about these challenges to authority in two statements which were provoked by the 1985 riots. (See Appendix 3)

The Church is clearly not the radical revolutionary community Jesus envisaged, but it is enlivened with many visionaries, prophets and people with long experience. Let us hope that, in common with all the authorities Jesus criticised, the church authorities will be prepared to listen and to serve as Jesus wanted.

9

Jesus Mixed With The Wrong People

'You can always judge people by the company they keep' is an old saying which many parents use to warn their children as they begin to spread their wings and make friends outside the family circle. Indeed, in 'society' in America and some middle class sections in this country, not only must one shun all demeaning company, but one must try very hard to be seen not only in the right company but in the right places too! Many Hollywood reputations have been made or lost along these lines.

In this country our class structure, though not so rigid as it used to be, still makes it difficult for ordinary working-class people and the aristocracy to mix, even if they wanted to. Snobbery on the other hand exists at all levels. If you live in a place like Brixton, and you want a job, it's always better to give your address as Stockwell. We have learned to our cost that Brixton is not a good address and to come from there is to be judged accordingly.

When people hear that I'm the Vicar of Angell Town they are usually amused and ask, 'Where exactly *is* Angell Town?' So I tell them that it's in the centre of Brixton. A shocked silence follows and slowly the words are choked out: 'Oh, it must be a real challenge for you mustn't it?' The headline in a local newspaper 'Local Vicar Supports Riots' sealed my doom. The headline was, of course, nonsense. It was a totally wrong conclusion drawn from a statement I had made about understanding the causes of the riots, which I still believe were mostly due to the problems of unemployment, lack of community facilities, financial squeezes and all the deprivation of inner city life. But it was easy to take my words, showing solidarity with the poor and needy, out of context. The result was that a local Conservative councillor threatened, in a headlined letter in the same paper, that she would kick me from John O'Groats to Lands' End. I accused her of being a middle class mugger and the letters went to and fro for a while. But, unsurprisingly, this made me persona non grata in local middle class circles!

As Musical Adviser to the BBC Songs of Praise programme I have been able to visit some of the most thriving churches in this country, to meet some genuinely interesting Christians, and to make music with all kinds of people. These occasions have endorsed traditional church Christianity and shown it at its best, but it has often been very difficult for me to suddenly switch language and mentality from Brixton to polite middle class suburbia. There is a particular kind of Brixton lifestyle and accompanying Brixtonese. Perhaps this is best described by saying that in Brixton there is a heightened consciousness about racist language, behaviour and concepts and all are openly criticised. The same goes for sexist language and women's issues and, to a lesser extent, gay language and issues. It is undoubtedly a highly politicised language peppered with all known 'ists' and 'isms' but it encourages a kind of awareness that ought to be shared among Christians if they are to be sensitive to the issues which can hurt people and divide our society. In this context a swear word, which some well-intentioned parents might threaten to wash out with the proverbial carbolic, can be less offensive than a racist or sexist joke; and the kind of Christian teaching which emphasises such minor details at the expense of good community relations has got its priorities wrong. It is better to direct energies against the greater problems, and this becomes an all-pervading influence in the inner city.

The sort of company you keep does rub off, then, but when we're all in this together that's not such a bad thing. I have learnt a great deal about minority needs and political awareness in Brixton that has influenced my thinking and changed me as a person.

In the popular imagination there are wrong places for vicars to be seen, and certain company that they are not expected to keep. All inner city areas have their places of doubtful reputation. When I first came to Brixton a pub was pointed out to me which was supposed to have a worldwide reputation for prostitution and drugs. There are still places like that even now in Brixton. It was this kind of reputation that led my parish clerk, a venerable Scots lady, to warn me in John Laurie's best ghost-story tones about another pub in the middle of my parish: 'Dunna gwa to the Angell—it's a terrrrrrible place.' Naturally enough I called there at my first opportunity. It was full of loud music, black people enjoying themselves, and the enticing smell of jerk pork. I felt like a total stranger. Over the years, as I have married some of those same people, conducted their funerals and baptised their children, I have got to know that part of the community very well, made good friends and, of course, found the warning to be unjustified. There are still those, however, who think that vicars ought not to mix with such company.

At the beginning of my ministry in Brixton ministering in pubs was important because there were few other places to meet people. Most of the parish was razed to the ground and wrapped in corrugated iron. People didn't like walking the derelict streets and wouldn't open their doors to visitors after dark, but they would pop round the corner to the pub, and I built up a good network of contacts in this way.

The British Public House is a part of our national heritage of which we can be justly proud. Pubs act as a community focus much in the way that churches do—the jokes about prayer books with handles show that the parallel has not gone unnoticed. Pubs are a great leveller, and there are not many other places where the old, the young and the middle-aged can meet on common ground. They are also good places for putting the world right, criticising the government, proving or disproving the existence of God, reincarnation and life after death; as well as approving or disapproving of the latest West Indies versus England cricket scores, Greenham Common women, Mrs Thatcher and nuclear arms.

Through all the contacts made in this way, I have got to know a great deal about Brixton and the kinds of problems people have to face every day, perhaps more than many people in my position. It has also enabled me to give help where it is most needed.

Jesus went much further in demonstrating his solidarity with the outcasts and the underprivileged of the world. The stereotyped image of a Jesus who never put a foot wrong is rubbished by the evidence in the Gospels. The Jesus of the gospels is a person who is quite prepared to behave in a revolutionary manner. He doesn't merely mix with the wrong kinds of people, he makes them his friends. He even eats with them in a society that took 'table-fellowship' very seriously. The passage after the call of Levi is a case in point:

'When Jesus was at table in his house, many bad characters—tax gatherers and others—were seated with him and his disciples; for there were many who followed him. Some doctors of the law who were Pharisees noticed him eating in this bad company, and said to his disciples, "He eats with tax gatherers and sinners!" Jesus heard it and said to them. "It is not the healthy that need a doctor, but the sick; I did not come to invite virtuous people, but sinners." ' (Mark 2:15, also Matt. 9:10; Luke 5:29)

The tax collectors (properly 'tax buyers') were regarded as traitors in Jewish society. They collaborated with the Roman occupying force and did their dirty work for them in the business of extracting taxes. Sinners may be regarded as many kinds of wrongdoers.

If we equate the Pharisees with the respectable middle classes, we begin to understand the enormity of Jesus' crime. It is unbelievable that he should mix with such low life and unbearable that he should even allow them into his intimate company. He couldn't have been worth much if he'd do a thing like that! Jesus explains his behaviour by pointing out that healthy people don't need doctors—but this is not enough for his critics. Jesus tells us that he has been accused of even more demeaning gaffes:

> 'For John came, neither eating nor drinking, and they say, "He is possessed". The Son of Man came eating and drinking, and they say, "Look at him! a glutton and a drinker, a friend of tax gatherers and sinners!" And yet God's wisdom is proved right by results.' (Matt. 11:18, also Luke 7:34)

This Jesus is a powerful figure in the way he overcomes such a putdown. In speaking and behaving in this way he puts his finger on one thing that people find very difficult to understand or to forgive—that it is possible to be godly, Christian and holy and *still* enjoy life to the full. The church has aggravated this tension. Somehow our institutionalised church has lost its relevance to ordinary people, and, as fewer people get married in church and fewer parents bring their babies to be baptised, it is fast becoming completely out of touch. For Jesus to be accused of being a glutton and a drinker, he must have kept some jolly company! He must also have had what is called the 'common touch' in order to mix with all kinds of people so easily. You wouldn't hear of the Archbishop of Canterbury being described in such a way. Yet doesn't this just prove the point. Our institutional church has got too far away from the early church risk-taking and dynamism which was disturbing the world order and threatening authority. The church of today is scared stiff of anything unconventional or of anyone 'rocking the boat'.

Jesus, in fact, was not merely rocking the boat, he was shaking the foundations! And if E.P. Saunders is right, then he was even more revolutionary than we have so far seen. The gospel picture that I hope I have been helping to recapture shows Jesus ministering to ordinary people, the poor and the outcasts. Many people have done the same, Christians or not. Can we really believe that this was enough to get him crucified? Certainly he would have ruffled a lot of feathers in high places but to such an extent that death was the only answer?

Jesus seems to have gone one dangerous step further. It wasn't just that the common people were included in Jesus' community, he actually welcomed the wicked. It is clear that Jesus included sinners but it is not clear that he required his followers to confess their sins and be forgiven. On the contrary he seems to have operated an all-comers policy, actually accepting people in their 'wicked' or 'lost' state. This seems to be endorsed by Luke's string of 'lost' stories: the Lost Sheep, the Lost Coin and the Lost or Prodigal Son. Thanks is given when the lost ones are welcomed back, but they are taken back unconditionally. Jesus' way of life, it would seem, was so open that the only condition was to follow him. This, if it is true, is clearly the greatest revolution of all. And it is echoed in other places. In Luke 14 Jesus gives instructions on how to throw a dinner party which I don't think would go down well in polite society.

> 'When you are having a party for lunch or supper do not invite your friends, your brothers, or other relations, or your rich neighbours; they will only ask you back again and so you will be repaid. But when you give a party, ask the poor, the crippled, the lame, the blind; and so find happiness.' (Luke 14:12)

Later Jesus tells a story about a big dinner party to which all the invited guests made excuses. The host got angry that all his important guests wouldn't come but his reaction was to go to the deprived and the oppressed.

> 'The host said, "Go out quickly into the streets and alleys of the town, and bring me in the poor, the crippled, the blind, and the lame." The servant said, "Sir, your orders have been carried out and there is still room." The master replied, "Go out on to the highways and along the hedgerows and make them come in; I want my house to be full." ' (Luke 14:21)

A similar story in Matthew takes this a stage further.

' "Go out to the main thoroughfares, and invite everyone you can find to the wedding." The servants went
out into the streets, and collected all they could find,
good and bad alike. So the hall was packed with
guests.' (Matt. 22:9)

Luke tells us about the down and outs who come to
Jesus' party, but the quotation from Matthew bears out
the case: Jesus invites good and bad alike, and they are
equally welcome, no strings attached.

The saying that pushes the case furthest and was guaranteed to upset those in authority and the religious
leaders is the most revolutionary of all. In making this
statement Jesus completely upsets the status quo and
turns the world order upside down. Jesus threatens the
chief priests and elders of the nation.

' "I tell you this: tax gatherers and prostitutes are
entering the Kingdom of God ahead of you. For when
John came to show you the right way to live, you did
not believe him, but the tax gatherers and prostitutes
did; and even when you had seen that, you did not
change your minds and believe him." ' (Matt. 21:31)

Here we have the main strands of Jesus' gospel preaching
as I have been trying to follow them through. He talks
about 'the right way to live', which I equate with the
Kingdom statements. To share this way of life is to
'change your minds', which I have equated with a change
of heart. The weight of the rest of Jesus' statement
almost suggests that unless we become like tax gatherers
or prostitutes we should not be able to be part of Jesus'
community. Well, it's not necessary for me to overstate
the case, Jesus' own language is forceful enough. And it
is in the force of his argument that we may find why the
authorities wanted him killed. He denied and threw in
their faces everything they stood for while pointing to
them as good examples of the lowest of the low.

It is impossible for us to escape the judgement of those
same words. They are an indictment on our own organised church, not just in this country. Leonardo Boff and

Gustavo Gutierrez have heavily criticised the Roman Catholic Church in their works on liberation theology and the Church of England has much to learn from their wisdom. The problem is that the church is not actually a church of the people, and certainly not of the oppressed and the outcast. It is rather a church of the privileged and it maintains rigid and protected hierarchies. Nor does the church seem at all inclined to repent! Those who try to speak out, like David Jenkins drawing attention to the plight of his mining families, are pilloried for their efforts. Even at the grassroots level, parish priests are tempted to minister to their faithful few, interpreting coming to the marriage feast as coming to church!— instead of reversing the parable and leaving their one sheep in the fold while they go and seek the other ninety nine! To the young, the poor, the criminal, the under-privileged, the unemployed, the black, the gay, the women, the church's message is all too often one of rejection, illustrated with images of privilege and the trappings of middle class respectability.

Jesus asks us to revolutionise our whole concept of 'the Church'. And there is hope in, of all places, the inner city. If Jesus was right, it is among the ordinary people, and the underprivileged, among the outcasts, the unem-ployed and the prostitutes that we may find the fertile soil for the nourishment and growth of the community of the followers of Jesus. This is a true revolution.

'And now I am sending down to you what the Father has promised. Stay in the city then, until you are clothed with the power from on high.' (Luke 24:49)

10

Jesus Wanted People To Be Free

'The slave has no permanent standing in the household, but the son belongs to it forever. If the Son sets you free, you will indeed be free.' (John 8:35)

In pastoral counselling we learn to work out and explore various aspects of relationships between people, and the insights gained can be valuable in other areas of life. One of the dangers of being a vicar is that one is prone to discover aspects of dependency in one's relationships. Vicars love to help people, but if one does things *for* other people instead of helping them to help themselves, they have to come back for more. This gives vicars a nice feeling of being needed, but a dependency has been set up because the person being helped comes to rely on that help as a prop—they become dependent on that help source and find it difficult to survive without it. As with training children, it is better for people to learn to cope with problems themselves, become more self-reliant, and wean themselves from the person who is helping them. This is, of course, not peculiar to vicars, it is a common aspect of relationships in all the helping professions.

If people learn an expertise—teaching, medicine etc.—they create a need for that expertise in their clients, (unless their clients already recognise their need of the service being offered):

You need to be taught/healed. I can teach/heal you. Therefore you need me.

Nevertheless your teacher or doctor also needs you or their expertise is invalidated. If nobody wants to be taught or healed, they're out of a job!

So you need your teacher or doctor and your teacher or doctor needs you to need him or her. This relationship is not only respectable, it is recognised by society as being not only acceptable but also beneficial. Still, a dependency is created and the two partners collude in playing out their roles in the teacher/pupil, doctor/patient relationships. At its furthest point this can become a master/victim or master/slave relationship. Even in popular speech we say that people are slaves to drugs, housework, the office and so on. We all experience dependency of one kind or another.

Dependency is not always bad, but, as I noted at the beginning, if people are not weaned from it at some stage it can lead to powerlessness or impotence because it strangles independence.

In our society the Welfare State has been under attack for this very reason. The argument runs that people have become so dependent on the state that they have lost the ability to help themselves, to show initiative, to be independent and to stand on their own two feet.

Significantly for Christians this has been discovered at a different level and expressed by liberation theologians in what has been called 'dependence theory'. This theory talks about whole groups of people, even nations, who have been dominated by other 'richer' or 'more successful' groups. Both capitalist and Marxist communist systems are open to criticism by this theory because both contain elements of dependency and domination. The capitalist criticism is more familiar to us. The wealthiest people, groups, companies, and countries dominate by reason of their wealth and power. They need to dominate a certain group in order to remain powerful, and the poor and needy collude in this dependency by continually coming to the richer and more powerful agents, cap in hand, asking for handouts or loans.

This is a familiar model even in our own commonwealth where the poorer nations—'third world' or 'developing'—have provided raw materials to be used by the more advanced economy in Britain. Specialisation in raw material production has led to disastrous situations in some countries. Take Jamaica, for instance, where bauxite rescued the economy for a short time until supplies ran out and the country had to fall back on sugar production. Unfortunately sugar is now being produced more cheaply in the EEC, so much so that Jamaica has to import cheap sugar and sell its own crop at a loss. This dependency policy is now wrecking the balance of world economies. Other casualties are Sri Lanka where tea workers still do not get an economic wage, or Ghana where raw cocoa was exported to Britain and chocolate imported much more expensively—leaving a whole economy dependent on the fluctuating price of cocoa!

Now these kinds of dependencies don't only work at national levels. They can also be found in relationships between inner and outer parishes. The Church of England is funded primarily through its collection plates. This is an extraordinary state of affairs, but it happens to be true. What it means is that suburban parishes, where more people go to church and therefore more money is put into the plate, are generally richer than inner city parishes. Churches pay a 'quota' to the diocese which goes to pay for vicars and curates, bishops and other diocesan functionaries, and for the various synods. This means that, although inner city widows may be giving their mites, most of the church's income comes from the richer middle class suburban and mainly white parishes. Small wonder if he who pays the piper calls the tune! And the tune therefore is usually a white middle class one.

A parish like mine in the centre of Brixton is populated by the unemployed, single parent families, children (there are six hundred children under the age of sixteen living on the estate next to my church) and old age pensioners. Indeed, when the diocesan financial advisers came to interview us about how to assess our quota, we didn't fit into even the lowest category. They just hadn't ever considered that a parish could contain so many 'disadvantaged' people. From this it may easily be realised that many inner city parishes cannot pay their own way, nor pay for their clergy or their expenses.

This once more causes a dependency situation in the relationship between the dioceses and the inner city parishes. In practice this means that inner city disadvantaged people, bearing more than their fair share of the problems of life, are also dependent on the generosity or otherwise of the richer white middle class congregations. On top of that it should be remembered that most of our clergy are white and middle class and find it hard to put themselves in the place of those who live in the inner city.

The result is that the inner city parishes, in a dependency relationship, are forever having to make a case for extra money in order to meet greater needs, for extra facilities, always going cap in hand, and always being treated as an exception to a white middle class rule which, of course, they did not make.

This rings many bells at a national level as well. It is this business of being made to feel dependent and delinquent and an exception to all the rules that has led to the volatile situation in many of our inner city areas.

It is difficult to find models which have tried to break out of the dependency syndrome. Marxism has tried but, paradoxically, Marxist theory is based on the disruption which occurs because of the separation and dependency caused between the middle class power holders and alienated working classes with no power. Marxism needs the dependency relationship to exist in order to inaugurate the revolutionary tension in the first place.

We have even tried in our local churches to set up an 'experimental' Brixton deanery. This has had some startlingly good results in helping us to discover more about our neighbouring Christians, as we have shared similar problems and felt the power of prayer for our common concerns—everything from leaks in the roof and a hostel for runaway kids, to trying to change the world! The irony is that we are totally dependent on both the money and the goodwill of the diocese to continue such work. We remain victims of our own situation. Still small mustard seeds have been known to grow and our plant has not reached its full height yet.

A modestly successful way to work with dependency situations between inner and outer parishes, and to help bridge the gaps, has been through twinning. Inevitably this means extra work for both parishes involved, but it does allow parishes to exchange ideas, to begin to understand each other better and for the richer parishes to know where their money is going.

We twinned up with St Margaret's Chipstead—a beautiful little Surrey village on a hill just off the A23. Christopher, the rector, has worked hard to keep links alive and we have done our bit in return, though with only two cars amongst the congregation it is not so easy for us to travel en masse. They have a population only about a quarter the size of ours, and the community is clearly much more settled. It is easy to make mistakes though. It was easy for them to be patronising—and it was easy for us to be too challenging and political, seeming to knock all middle class values. But we have had some good times and met some people who have understood and wanted to help.

One of the funniest incidents was when their youth club came to see us. We'd promised them a trip to a typical friendly Brixton pub where they could meet everyone, hear some good reggae music and have a good time. It would be the one night when a beer bottle suddenly flew through the air and almost hit one of them on the head, neatly demolishing a window behind her! Still, it didn't stop them coming back for more, and they began to realise that there are places in Brixton that are almost like a village community.

If we are able to get over these kinds of teething troubles, there is plenty of scope for changes of heart and growth in the way of the gospel—the kind of revolution that Jesus envisaged.

Outer parishes are usually strong enough to run themselves, and yet they attract more clergy. There needs to be self-sacrifice and a greater sharing of ministry with lay people who, on the whole, are used to organising and running things, and have much to give in terms of the kinds of basic help many of our inner cities need. There needs to be an even greater sharing of resources—especially financial resources—so that inner city people can build up their ministries and witness, having been freed from some of the everyday anxieties which plague them.

A leaking roof, for example, is a problem common to all churches wherever they are situated. In an outer church, a fundraising campaign would be launched, and after several months the work would be put in hand. In the inner city it would be an insurmountable problem. It's almost impossible to raise money through fundraising campaigns and there are so many other problems which have to be solved first—yet another church break-in and burglary for instance, more windows to be boarded up (it's a waste of time trying to repair them, another stone will come through the same day), yet another gas or electricity bill to face, another old lady got mugged: can we help out?—that the roof will simply be the last straw, and may well lead to the demise of the whole building because there will be no money forthcoming for its repair.

Most of our young, up and coming families and couples move out to the suburbs as soon as they can. This means that much of the lay talent and ability nurtured by us, grows to fruition in the outer churches. It would be helpful if that kind of ability could be channelled back to us to help with fundraising, combatting unemployment, dealing with government and local government officials and red tape. I'm sure that Jesus would approve of this kind of sharing of abilities and gifts. But it shouldn't be left to us in the inner city to tell the outer churches what to do. It would be much more refreshing if, instead of waiting for us to come and ask for help, they took an interest in inner city issues and problems, offered help and pestered us to find what they could do. This could be the kind of growing, sharing and learning experience from which we all could benefit.

My main fear is that some people might leave. When we all started shaking hands at the peace, the more 'respectable' members of our congregation left. They didn't want to shake hands with other people. They didn't even seem to want to get to know the other people in the congregation. Maybe the people in the outer churches wouldn't want to come quite so close to those who live in Brixton—maybe it would bring their religion down to earth with too much of a bump! Much to my delight, when a large group of my congregation accompanied me to my old college, Jesus in Cambridge, where I was preaching, after the initial culture shock was over both those at the college and those from Brixton enjoyed themselves immensely and began what may prove to be a fruitful relationship.

'If a man says, "I love God", while hating his brother, he is a liar. If he does not love the brother whom he has seen, it cannot be that he loves God whom he has not seen.' (1 John 4:20)

It seems hard for Christians to love their brothers and sisters in places like Brixton, however, and the credibility gap between the inner city churches and suburban Christians remains very wide.

Recently eight vicars in Brixton took on two or three weeks extra work: extra meetings both among themselves and with their churchpeople, and extra time with TV producers and filming crews, trying to explain and to help them understand what the churches are trying to do in Brixton. When the 'Brixton Eight' was shown we felt that it was a modest and truthful programme if a little short on theology. We all came over as being very middle class, which, of course, we are, and we were sorry that our lay people were not featured at all. We talked about all our different imaginative rebuilding schemes for the optimal use of our various church premises. I think we showed just how creative inner city people are, and how skilled they have become at the best kind of husbandry of their resources. We described how good our local police persons are, especially those who pound the beat. But we also tried to explain about the problems—the estates, the unemployment, the hopelessness and lack of future for our young people, and the rest of the difficulties which prevailed up to and during the riots, and which still continue.

Some people reacted with understanding, perhaps for the first time. But others sent letters, anonymously of course, from places like Epsom, full of personal insults, accusing us of 'making trouble' and worse. Coming as it did after a searching, positive, critical but encouraging attempt to evaluate the Brixton churches, it seemed especially cruel and made us feel as though the gap between inner and outer areas might never be bridged.

In the inner city we can describe our hurt but we have no monopoly on ways of improving the situation. Jesus calls us all to repent. Suburban people in strong parishes also need to examine their attitudes and be prepared to change their opinions. Please do not condemn all those of us who live in the inner city simply because we live there. Do not believe that we are all criminals, muggers, rioters and worse. Instead, try to come alongside us and share some of the issues that concern us. Jesus expected us to help each other, but you cannot help people unless you make an effort to understand their true needs.

'Lord, when was it that we saw you hungry or thirsty or a stranger or naked or ill or in prison, and did nothing for you? And he will answer, I tell you this: anything you did not do for one of these, however humble, you did not do for me.' (Matt. 25:44)

Some things we can all do:

1. In order to do things for suffering and underprivileged people there has to be a steady and concerted commitment to change. If this is not coming through the governmental machinery of this country, then we must ask all Christians in the Church of England to commit themselves to change. This may well mean radical change. Redressing the imbalances of wealth between the richer and poorer nations of the world to bring about equality will necessarily make the rich people poorer. This is one of the costs of following Jesus.

When we highlight the injustice of the plight of our inner cities, we are often told that we need to seek reconciliation. But reconciliation can only occur when there has been conciliation in the first place. Those who live in the inner city need to be given the means to become more independent. They need to be able to earn their own living. They need to be free to choose their own housing. Above all they need to feel that they are able to contribute positively to society instead of continually being dismissed as a bunch of drop-outs and rejects. Think about inner city people positively. Explore ways of investing in and improving the inner city, help to provide jobs, offer know-how, but above all refuse to allow those in authority to use the inner cities as dumping grounds for all their problems. Lobby MPs, write to newspapers, talk to local bureaux of commerce and industry, involve women's groups—WIs, Mothers' Unions. This extra degree of politicisation will help to make us all more responsible for social justice and the future shape of our society, threatened as it is by the imbalance of poverty and need in inner city areas. Jesus said, 'Stay in the city until you are clothed with the power from on high.' (Luke 24:49)

2. Do not allow politicians to play a political game using the inner cities as the ball. We need a concerted political effort from all parties to redress the wrongs inflicted on inner city areas. Liverpool and Lambeth are held up for ridicule in the present political game, but it is the people who suffer. We should not allow those who profess to be our political leaders, and spend *our* money, to make inner city people political scapegoats. Demand accountability through, for instance, your parish council for Government spending, and invite your MP to explain what he or she and parliament are doing about public spending on inner city areas. Do the same with your local councillors. Remind them of Jesus' words in Matthew 25.

3. Visit those in prison and be appalled at the conditions first-hand. And, just as importantly, examine our whole society's attitude to problem people. Much has been done in mental hospitals in the last decades to save people with difficulties from being locked away. Equally, those who do wrong need to be helped to repent and start a new life—our present prison system in no way assists this. Out of sight is not out of mind, and the prison system is very expensive on manpower and resources.
Look more carefully at community service orders and how they could be used more effectively. Research what is happening in other countries like Holland and Scandinvaia.

Work out positive ways of helping—do not simply seek retribution as this is against Jesus' way of life: 'Lord, how often am I to forgive my brother if he goes on wronging me? As many as seven times? Jesus replied, "I do not say seven times; I say seventy times seven." ' (Matt. 18:21)

Look out other passages which show Jesus' attitude to those who do wrong and try to work out what it all means for us today. Remember that Jesus welcomed all into his community, good and bad alike. We have not yet discovered the full significance of his teaching and its revolutionary effect on the reform of our legal, judicial and penal systems. Jesus said: 'He has sent me to proclaim release for prisoners'; and, 'We forgive all who have done us wrong.'

4. Read *Faith in the City*, the Report of the Archbishop's Commission on the Inner Cities. Use as a Lent Course and then work out what your church collectively, and you individually, can actually *do* in response. Remember that no effective steps have been taken by the government to alleviate unemployment during the last seven years. Indeed unemployment, especially among the 16-25 age group and among black people, has almost tripled since the 1981 riots.

Remember that the withdrawal of financial support from many inner city areas (rate capping) has drastically reduced services to old people, families, young people, and those at risk. Remember that real poverty has increased while the average wage has risen. Remember that many people are not consciously aware of their racism. Jesus said, 'Feed my sheep'.

5. Do *not* read the *Sun*, the *Daily Mail*, the *Daily Express*. Jesus said, 'Take care that no one misleads you'.

6. See what can be done through church schools and diocesan boards of education to look at the future and to help our children feel positive about it. The crying need is for the sixteen to twenty age group. Examine the need for

Sixth Form Colleges. Help that group of no-hope young people who are at present hostages to fortune when they should be preparing to be tomorrow's leaders. Jesus said: 'Let the children come to me—don't try to stop them; for the kingdom of God belongs to such as these.'

7. Recommend that money be poured into the inner city. Help with fund-raising. This does not mean Beetle Drives and jumble sales, though of course every little helps. It really means finding way of raising thousands and millions of pounds to refloat the inner cities. Jesus said: 'Is there a father among you will offer his son a stone when he asks for bread, a snake when he asks for fish, or a scorpion when he asks for an egg?'

8. Work out possible new lifestyles for the future. There is plenty of room for think-tank work along these lines—so few people are doing it. Work out what having a three-day week might mean. Discuss the place of the arts and leisure industries, the service and catering industries in the future, and how the financial industries can be developed so that wealth is shared more equitably. Explore the implications of education throughout life instead of between the ages of five and sixteen. Work out projections for a greatly developed education industry. Anticipate what changes to the structure of our whole society this would necessitate. Jesus said: 'Ask and you will receive; seek and you shall find; knock and the door will be opened.'

9. Work out whether Christian inputs to all this would be sufficient, or whether we need to revolutionise society into a totally Christian context. How could we effect a more equitable allocation of resources not only in this country, but also in the world? How can we encourage the better development of people's talents, especially the squandered gifts of people in the inner cities?

Remember the important work of the Quakers, their garden cities and co-operatives in this field. Read about Robert Owen. Visit Bournville. Find out about Josiah Wedgewood. To see how you can help developing countries write to the Intermediate Technology Group, 9 King Street, London WC2 for an information pack. 'You are a light for the world', Jesus said, 'And you must shed light among your fellows, so that, when they see the good you do, they may give praise to your Father in heaven.'

10. Pray.

11

Jesus Taught Us To Pray

One of the great harms we Christians have done to our religion is to separate body and spirit, secular and sacred. Every Moslem will tell you that his religion is his way of life. Hindus have their shrines in corners of their sitting rooms and life moves easily from friendly chat into prayer and ceremonial and then eating together. Judaism has become more stylised but the questions and answers which have to be made at the family Passover meal indicate that a distinction between the world and spirituality is not easily made.

It is also extraordinary when you realise what has happened in, for instance, the world of music. While Christianity genuinely dominated our culture and lifestyle for many centuries there was no great distinction between sacred and secular music. Choral settings of the Latin Mass in the fifteenth and sixteenth centuries, for instance, were often based not on 'sacred' plainsong but on 'secular' melodies like The Western Wind or L'Homme Armé. In the main order of things, everything was sacred. Similarly while the church dominated life it was also impossible to separate religion and politics. Archbishop Thomas à Becket was also Lord Chancellor of England.

It was mainly the Reformation which pushed spirituality into private individual corners away from daily life. The numbers of Protestant and Catholic martyrs in the late Tudor period made it a matter of survival to privatise your religious observances! Subsequent economic and commercial developments leading to the industrial revolution emphasised the separation. Increasingly the church seemed to be offering an escape from the world, a place where we could be holy and recharge our batteries before we plunged back into the fray. This remains the state of mind of many churchgoers and nominal Christians today. I like to call it the Ark mentality. The church is seen as the escape vessel where we can all be safe against the storms and ravages of the sea of life.

This was not Jesus' way. He involved himself in the whole of life and with those people involved in the more difficult aspects of life—so much so that he was criticised for being too worldly. I believe that Jesus' down-to-earth gospel needs a response from the church, and from individual Christians, which ought to be equally effective at a political and an institutional level, as well as at a pastoral and spiritual level. Above all we should resist the temptation to offer the false security of an escapist Christianity. Unfortunately many of the charismatic, pentecostal and black church movements have become so introspective that they are in danger of falling into the ark mentality trap.

It is well known that vocations to contemplative and religious orders are falling, just as they are to the priesthood. Some people would say that this is a sign of our ungodly times—that society is becoming more secularised and that we are moving further and further from God. But, looked at another way, it could be seen as a healthy sign that people are actually becoming more life-affirming in the sense that they do not wish to cut themselves off from the world. They are choosing rather to explore their God-given gift of life as widely as possible. From this point of view, the narrowly religious life looks like an escape from reality.

Charismatics and pentecostals claim rises in their membership and believe that they are offering what people most need in an age that glorifies human achievement to such an extent that spirituality is neglected. While I recognise that pentecostalism is clearly scriptural, there is as yet no evidence that it provides much more than a fashionable experience, a view endorsed by Ronald Knox in *Enthusiasm*, his study of such movements in history.

The main danger is that these byways of Christianity are simply ways to escape from life and that they are based on a dual concept of human nature, characterised in many eastern religions. The unique quality of Christianity is found in the incarnation—not in the sense that God dressed up in human flesh, as so many of our hymns encourage us to believe, but, much more challengingly, that God was recognised in Jesus, in his life, his crucifixion and resurrection. This is Christianity's great revolutionary contribution to religious thought and experience. But its full significance can only be appreciated if we see that life and spirituality are not only interdependent but one and the same thing. A Christian should work out his or her spirituality trying to live the life that Jesus wanted. As Christians our God thoughts, our care for each other, the quality of love which is powerful beyond the confines of time and place, are all found in the working out of our life together.

I often hear people say that the world is such a terrible place that they cannot find God there. It is sometimes difficult to find the God dimension in the existence we all share, but we must remember that God was acting in its creation and that he loved it so much that he sent his Son. It is a pity that so many of us are shy of talking about our own private 'spirituality'. Similarly we aren't always aware how much other people's prayers affect us. But we can sometimes feel and be glad of the power of other people praying for us. When we all pray in church for someone who is ill, when we know that prayers are being offered all over the world in the face of catastrophe, there is a great feeling of power in that creative action.

At a simple human level though, if only ordinary people could be brave enough to share their prayers and their ideas about God, all too often the exclusive domain of a few specialised theologians, we could find and understand the power of God in life. This sharing activity would be more enlightening and helpful in living our spirituality than the stultifying membership of a small exclusive cult or ecclesiastical 'movement' could ever be. It seems to me that just as God prompted all Jesus' thoughts and actions, and just as Jesus seemed constantly to be in touch with God, so we should be able to think and act always with God in mind. I hasten to add that this is not intended to mean that we have to keep in touch with Head Office, making sure that we don't do anything to displease the Boss—that is a middle class image if ever there was one! I mean it much more in the Old Testament sense of covenant and close friendship, in the knowledge of the love, support and power of God to guide and help us.

I believe that it is in this kind of way that Jesus was able to speak and act as confidently as he did, while fully aware of the revolutionary effect of his words and actions.

When we turn to his words on prayer it is not surprising to find that, as usual, they are simple and direct, and yet they get to the very heart of the matter and turn the world upside down.

Luke's gospel introduces the Lord's Prayer in this way: 'Once in a certain place, Jesus was at prayer. When he ceased, one of his disciples said, "Lord teach us to pray, as John taught his disciples." ' (Luke 11:1)

There is a longer introduction in Matthew's gospel, mostly warning us not to parade our religion or draw attention to our praying. His last injunction is: 'In your prayers do not go babbling on like the heathen, who imagine that the more they say the more likely they are to be heard' (Matt. 6:7). I'd better make sure that warning is heeded by some pentecostal preachers I have heard who frequently assert that 'the more prayers are sent up to heaven, the more blessings are poured down'!

Many Christians are puzzled by the different 'versions' of the Lord's Prayer. There are basically two versions in popular use, both a kind of harmonised version of the prayer as it is found in both Matthew and Luke, ending with the familiar doxology which is not found in the earliest manuscripts. The older version comes from the 1662 Book of Common Prayer. The more modern version was first worked out by the International Consultation on English Texts and found its way, slightly altered, into our Alternative Service Book. The versions in Matthew and Luke are different again—the Lord's Prayer is not found in the Gospels of Mark or John.

In keeping with my belief in the directness and simplicity of Jesus' teaching, I'd like us to look at the most radical version:

'When you pray say:
"Father, your name be hallowed;
Your kingdom come.
Give us each day our daily bread,
And forgive us our sins,
for we too forgive all who have done us wrong.
And do not bring us to the test." ' (Luke 11:2)

The most significant word which sets the whole tone for Jesus' teaching about our relationships with God is the first word: 'Father'. In Matthew 14:36, and in Romans 8:15 and Galatians 4:6, there is a special Aramaic word quoted in the text. Aramaic was the language Jesus actually spoke. The word which is translated as father is 'Abba'. Paul tells us that he sees us all coming to share in 'sonship' so that we can all call God 'Abba! Father!' This translation loses its full significance because the true sense of the word is found in baby language, very much like 'Dadda' or 'Daddy'. Suddenly a whole world of revolutionary thinking is borne in on us in this one expression. No longer is God a remote being above and beyond us all. No longer do we need to fear him as in the Old Testament. Nor, and this is where our own language gets in the way, do we any longer need to address God as 'thou': the ancient word, which used to be a familiar usage as in French, has for too long pushed God into a position far too remote and separate from us all.

Jesus sweeps away centuries of tradition with his simple word 'Daddy'. He makes us feel that God is so close to us that we can call on him in the most intimate of terms; he tells us to pray in this way. With one little word he brings us all closer to God than we could ever have imagined. His revolutionary directness also cancels centuries of church teaching on intermediaries, whether priests or saints, between ourselves and God. Each of us has a hotline to God, unconditionally. It seems such a tragedy that for centuries the church has lost this great significance of Jesus' teaching on prayer.

'Your name be hallowed' is not simply an expression of respect. If that is all it were, then it would have the effect of distancing God again. This expression comes out of Jesus' Jewishness. The *name* of God was so holy that at one stage it was even forbidden to speak it. God's 'name' stood for God himself, but it was even more than that. Mention of the holy name of God was actually an invocation of God's presence. Jesus asks us to do the same. 'Your Kingdom come', takes us straight back to Jesus' original proclamation in Mark 1, with the emphasis not only on his personal message about the initiation of his community (the Kingdom) but also on the inclusion of all of us in that community. More than that, I believe, Jesus asked us to pray in this way to motivate *us*, to energise us, into helping and working to bring about his community.

'Give us each day our daily bread.' The word for 'daily bread' is not easy to translate—and the alternative given in the New English Bible 'bread for the morrow' doesn't actually clarify anything. Matthew has 'today' instead of 'each day', which I prefer because it underlines the urgency of Jesus' message, but neither version affects the main message very much. Whatever the differences, the direct request to God to feed us is perfectly clear. When we all pray this prayer together, however, the weight of responsibility becomes shared as God enables each of us to obtain our daily bread. We must share what we have. In my own prayer life I mentally link this passage with a sharp rejoinder made by Jesus, to his disciples, when they wanted to send the people away hungry since they didn't know how to give food to all of them. Jesus says: 'Give them something to eat yourselves.' (Luke 9:13) It is this petition which links up so closely with the injunction to feed the hungry in Matthew 25. Right at the heart of Jesus' prayer we find that his concern is for a just distribution of resources throughout the world. How real it is in this time of great famines and how real is our responsibility to give them all something to eat ourselves.

One way to involve people and help them to share their concern is by doing a 'Feed the World' service with local churches. Appendix 1 gives an example of such a service, which I hope may be of use. It represents a way of extending prayer into life, meditating on all our concerns both in words and in music. And the final agape brings everyone together as they literally share the bread. I believe that services like these are examples of 'doing prayer'. They help us to earth our spirituality and enable us to feel that the active sharing of our concerns is an extension of simple intercession.

'And forgive us our sins, for we too forgive all who have done us wrong. Once more Jesus stresses the importance of forgiveness and repentance. His forgiveness is unconditional. In Jesus' own community all are equal and we must all forgive each other, just as our Daddy forgives us, not seven times but seventy times seven. (Matt. 18:22)

'And do not bring us to the test.' It is to the regret of all Christians that our society has not yet been able to face up to the responsibilities of institutionalised forgiveness. Repeated calls for the death penalty (institutionalised murder) and harder sentences for criminals (institutionalised violence) make it all too clear that many people are not able to appreciate the benefits that a Christian system of forgiveness could bring to all our lives individually and corporately. This is an area where Christians need to do much more to bring about Jesus' clearly worded but ultimately revolutionary challenge: 'We too forgive all who have done us wrong.'

It is unfortunate that the ASB version of the Lord's prayer has restored 'temptation'. But this passage is notoriously difficult, and it may be that we cannot recover exactly what Jesus meant. It is true that Jewish history in the Old Testament often shows how God tests people. The story of Job is probably enough in itself to support this notion, but it doesn't help us to understand Jesus' meaning any better. If we are talking in the context of inaugurating a new age, or a new way of life, which I believe is what Jesus intended, then we may be talking in terms of the Last

Judgement. If the new community is happening now, Jesus is asking God (and, therefore, so are we) that we should not be subjected to a final judgement before we have a chance to be allowed to share in this new community. What we must do is found in the rest of Jesus' teaching about changing our hearts and minds, and having a new revolutionary attitude to the world and other people in this new age. The longer version in Matthew doesn't help much more and the reading 'the evil one' would seem to take us back to the story of Job with its personification of evil.

In this way, in spite of passages which are difficult to understand, we find the heart of Jesus' revolutionary message encapsulated in the prayer he handed on to us, including a revelation about our relationship with God.

Other references to prayer in the gospels are often recorded words of Jesus praying alone. These we may take as we wish, and they no doubt reflect much of the spirit of Jesus' teaching. Since he made so much of being alone on these occasions we can discount eavesdroppers and short of secretly tape-recording him, we cannot know how his words were handed on. Perhaps they were composed in the spirit of words Jesus had used on other occasions.

There are two other important passages which extend our appreciation of Jesus' view of life and spirituality.

'You have learned that they were told, "Love your neighbour, hate your enemy." But what I tell you is this: love your enemies and pray for your persecutors.' (Matt. 5:43)

Jesus refers to a saying from Leviticus 19:18, that would be most familiar to a Jew. As usual, he wants to take the middle class adherence to the observance of the law yet one stage further. In *his* community it is no longer enough just to love your neighbour. In fact he turns the whole traditional concept on its head and introduces a revolutionary idea: you have to love your enemy. The added instruction to pray for your persecutors is a natural extension which would have been sensitive and realistic to the early Christian martyrs.

The demand Jesus makes on his followers is such that it would, lived out to the full, change the world. It is sad, and to our continual shame, that Christians have not taken his demand either literally or seriously enough. There could be no debates about nuclear war, or even 'conventional arms', if this were the case. It is something we all still have to learn, but it supports my contention that Jesus had a practical working spirituality for us all to follow. He actually meant what he said.

The true weight he gave to the power of prayer in such an everyday spirituality is revealed in the last passage I should like to draw your attention to: 'Whatever you ask for in prayer, believe that you have received it and it will be yours.' (Mark 11:24)

In Jesus' community, prayer, both individual and communal, will bring about all that is necessary for the good of all.

It is this confidence in the power of prayer that we need to bring to the prayers in our own services as well as in our personal prayer times. When we pray for things together, whether it's for people who are sick, for peace in troubled areas, for those taking exams, for the old lady who got mugged yesterday, for our governments, for the hungry, or any of the other matters which crowd our thoughts each day, in our church communities we can feel the extra strength our shared concern gives us all.

In this way prayers in church, rather than 'bringing the world in' actually take us out into the world, empowering us to change it armed with all the prayers, thoughts, love and strength God gives us and we give one another. In this may be found the foundation of true worship. It is through these means that Jesus expected us to gain our inspiration to put his words into action, to put right the wrongs in the world and to bring in his revolution.

12

Jesus Brought Life In All Its Fullness

When someone composes a piece of music, the bare notes on the page mean very little until they are performed—clothed, brought to life, moulded and changed by the performers, and, most of all, made human. In this way everyone is involved, both in the collective consciousness of experiencing the music and in the practical performance: performers, audience and composer thus share in the conception and birth of the created work and are necessary to make it live.

Writing and producing a play is similar. Rather like Pirandello's *Six Characters*, in order for a play to live there has to be a partnership involving all concerned. The written script is just the beginning. Even when all the actors are primed and directed, and the designers briefed, if they only do exactly as they are directed the play will not take on a life of its own. The designer's artistic and creative flair should take off from the brief and not be proscribed by it. Similarly, the fact that the actors are going to do their own thing, sometimes in spite of the director ('I'll show him!') and sometimes because they are skilled in their craft and can do more than the director expected, means that the production will grow and become more exciting. Although it is energised by the producer/director, all the other people involved bring their own gifts to build up the corporate energy and create something more exciting than any one person in the team could possibly have done.

Because of my involvement in music and drama, I am

132

familiar with this dynamic and creative process. Sometimes, I think of God like a super producer, directing us to a certain extent, but expecting all of us to use our gifts to make his creation more exciting. Unfortunately, the church in history seems to have responded in an escapist way—hoping to preserve the few who are virtuous and leaving the rest to the flood! As followers of Jesus, we need to be more positive in our attitudes, helping people to feel valued as part of a great creative process, to trust in God's love, and enabling them to explore the whole of life. We need to adopt a more hopeful and searching attitude if we are to help *all* people to the fuller life Jesus wanted. Inevitably, as in big business, that means using the right kind of entrepreneurial ability and taking *risks*, and having the faith that God will see things through to a creative conclusion.

The most persuasive way forward at present may be seen in the down-to-earth roots of Latin-American liberation theology. The 'base ecclesial communities' in South America are best described by Leionardo Boff in his book *Church, Charism and Power*. This is a revolutionary way forward—which is why he has been in so much trouble with the Vatican—because it sweeps away much of the agglomerated ecclesiastical clutter of centuries. This is a grass-roots movement made up of lower class people who are not only at the base of society but are also at the base of the church and its structures. The communities are usually made up of fifteen to twenty families who meet once or twice a week to read the Bible and share their common problems in the hope that the Gospel might help them find ways of solving those problems. Their origin lies partly in the shortage of clergy which means that lay people have to take on pastoral roles and, at times, priestly functions. The people make up their own prayers and work out a priority for the jobs and problems to be tackled. Boff sees this activity as recreating the church and causing people to make an active option for the poor and the oppressed and for their liberation. Everyone voices his or her own opinion and is given enough space to do it in. Collectively the group, in sharing its problems and its abilities, is increasingly able to take on the social system at various political levels and deal with specific problems like schooling, water supply, electricity and hospitals. Everyone works towards true brotherhood and sisterhood, over and above family ties, and all share in the jobs to be done for the good of all. Although all are equal, each person is allowed to explore what they are best at and bring his or her gifts to enrich and benefit the community as a whole.

I hope that all this rings bells and bears out much that I have been trying to identify in earlier chapters. I believe that it does represent a significant step in the direction of the way of life Jesus wanted—the formation of a true Christian community. It certainly sounds familiar to many of us who live in inner city areas. Where ordinary people can be brought together and motivated, there is no doubt that the Jesus Revolution can begin to happen in the wealth of hitherto ignored human potential which is to be found in the groups of people who are not normally allowed their say. We have certainly found this ourselves in our Brixton Deanery experiment and the excitement of it all is that, whether you look at Jesus' jubilee speech (Luke 4), the sharing in common of the disciples (Acts 2), or Jesus' own demands in the Beatitudes, this whole approach to Christianity seems to get right to the heart of the Gospel.

There is a story about the bumble bee. Apparently it has such a tiny wingspan for such a huge body that, by the laws of aerodynamics, it could not possibly fly. Luckily the bumble bee, never having been forced to learn about aerodynamics, doesn't know this and consequently, not only does it fly perfectly well, it makes a little honey too!

I often think that inner city Christians and churches are rather like the bumble bee. All the pressures are against the survival of churches in these areas, yet not only do our groups of Christians survive, we also manage to create a great deal of good feeling and support among our congregations, and spearhead new developments in Christianity into the bargain.

One of the main troubles is that when so much energy

has to be put into mere day to day survival, there is little left for the exploration of the fullness of life. The inner areas need help and have been asking for it for a long time. It is very slow in coming. Meanwhile self-help schemes have involved the shared use or alternative use of many churches and their buildings. This is preferable to demolition because, although in theory Christians are perfectly able to worship in schools, halls, front rooms or fields, people still like to identify with their local church building and worship centre. When I first came to my present parish, the church was the only building still standing, and it represented the only way of letting people feel they could belong or that there was any continuity with the past, in a wilderness of corrugated iron and desolation. The fact the church also offers a huge architectural space is often an exhilarating experience for people who are used to being trapped in overcrowded cubes most of the time.

Helping people to find a point in life is an important and at times all-pervading problem, especially when it seems as if the world is against them, but the help given must be practical. A Ghanaian friend once said to me that there is little point in talking to a person about spiritual food if his belly is empty. The continual run-down of local authority services through governmental cuts and rate-capping, coupled with continually rising unemployment and the feeling of being discriminated against, has left all but the bookies and the drugs barons feeling impotent and unable to use initiative. We shall be reaping a harvest of tragedy for years to come from the closing down of the GLC.

Nevertheless, some local church initiated projects have begun to show the way. The indefatigable Greta Brooks, who is a Quaker, with her police station lay-visiting teams sponsored by Brixton Council of Churches, has already proved a valued practical help. Agencies like Stockwell Good Neighbours and Help '71 use teams of volunteers to help people in all kinds of practical ways, not least in providing cheap clothing and furniture. At a different level, the Brixton Festival, which I was pleased to help found, is now well established as a feast of music, local talent and of course traditional West Indian food. At least it has helped people into an awareness of the good things life can offer that they can be successful at themselves.

It is in the realm of the arts: music, dance, theatre and all the allied creative interests, that life can be enriched for everyone. You don't have to be rich to sing—but it is difficult for people to believe in a more fulfilled life if their present existence and possible future are under threat.

I was born just after the first atomic bombs were dropped on Hiroshima and Nagasaki, so the nuclear threat has haunted the entire forty years of my life. People are frankly terrified of the mushroom cloud and of the fact that our entire world could be destroyed in seconds at the push of a button over which we have no influence or control whatsoever. This causes people to think and worry about the end of the world as they have at no other time, since the immediate period after Jesus' death. This feeling permeates all age groups, and the urgency and the sense of living in the last times have alarming effects. Our young people in particular, already alienated by unemployment and other economic factors, seem unable to find hope or motivation in life, and many familiar mores of society are being obviated. If God is not dead then he seems to have deserted the world.

Christianity, as I hope I have been able to show in this study, has much to say about all this and should be able to offer some hope. The seeds of community lifestyle have been sewn, but those who wish to follow Jesus must take their example from him.

Those in authority in this country and the world should not be allowed to duck their responsibilities. To bring life in all its fullness to all people should be their constant desire and aim. This involves economic equalisation and a sharing of world resources as Jesus asked us. Governments ought to take on a greater responsibility for the poor and starving of the world. World economic systems which help rich nations but result in disasters in poorer nations need, in the name of humanity, to be completely changed, and this is the responsibility of the wealthy nations. There must be a way to share out the riches of the world so that everyone can benefit. We have seen how sanctions from all the world can have an impact on an immoral régime like South Africa's, though it is to our shame that our own government did not join in. It must be possible for Christians all over the world to influence their governments to bring equality of opportunity to developing nations.

As Christians we have an important responsibility to try to change the hearts and minds of our own government and politicians. Jesus called on us all to share in his revolution. We must do this first by trying to create what has been called social justice. The poor, the suffering, the oppressed, the powerless must all be helped and given the resources to help themselves into equality of life and opportunities. This can never be done by cuts in education, hospital services, housing, old people's welfare, grants to the inner city, and local democracy. Nor can it ever happen when, in a context of chronic unemployment, so-called 'top' people, who are no more socially productive than refuse collectors, (and possibly less so), are awarded decorative increments in pay which represent four times the total annual wage paid to junior teachers, nurses and vicars.

Some voices in the church have been heard—even in the House of Lords—speaking out against this scandal. Hospitals and education were for many centuries a prime concern of the church. It may be, as in local government, that things have been going so wrong since Christians relinquished responsibility that we ought to reclaim these areas and once more create ways of helping the old and the sick. We could certainly do a much better job with what remains of our church schools to ensure that they are teaching children a living faith and the Jesus way of life instead of a vapid moral background based on double values. Much, much more needs to be done, in the name of Christ.

Can the inner cities ever be helped?—aren't they just a bottomless well? There will always be sceptics who talk about throwing good money after bad, but in fact inner city people can be very resourceful and there is usually much to show for even small amounts of cash if they are channelled into the right community groups. It is easy to stifle this kind of initiative and it requires careful nurture for the best kind of growth. The frustrations of red tape and complicated procedures are themselves often enough to choke such initiative at birth. But those involved in the middle class structures of society could all help: procedures could be simplified, communications could be improved by taking the time to explain things more carefully to people, and able middle class people could use their own initiative to challenge the system from within. Disadvantaged people and those used to the system could then join together in the creative process and all could share in the growth and new life which would result.

The people of Brent, especially the young black people, have shown a wonderful initiative with their imaginative transformation of some old bus sheds into a multi-faceted resource for their community. The people who live in the East-End docklands have put together a community-based plan for a massive sports centre, marina, shops and other facilities to bring back life to a dying area—though at the present time this initiative has been smashed down in favour of a Stolport which could only aid rich businessmen.

In Brixton there have been many schemes and they have had varying success rates. I shall describe the one I have been most involved with. Some ten years ago, after we had tried all the usual youth club type activities using my church premises, it became clear that 'keeping them off the streets' was not enough for our young people who had no places or facilities in the area to call their own. I talked with youth leaders, young people, tenants associations, social services people, the police, churches and anyone else interested. These meetings eventually came up with something of a revolutionary concept in youth work. It was to be directive; it was to be disciplined; it was to be creative; but, above all, it had to bring a quality of fulfilment and enjoyment to the young people. Hopefully this would not only help them to feel that life was worth living, but also that a good quality of life was accessible.

The creative arts seemed to offer all of this, the possibility of being open to spiritual values as well as work at a practical level, and so the idea of the Angell Centre was born. It would provide a large studio for theatre, dance and music, and several other rooms, office, classroom, changing rooms, library, coffee bar/restaurant, and small hall for meetings and concerts. It would not be run as a community centre, open to all with money enough to book rooms for their own organisations, but as a college, with a director and tutors on hand to take well-disciplined classes to teach the children new abilities and develop the gifts they already had.

Agreement to fund this plan under the inner city programme was given eight years ago—but we are still waiting for the money to implement the plan, since changing governments and different urban planning policies have meant constant review and whittling down of the original idea. It is easy to see how even powerful and shared initiative can be lost under such a minefield of procedure.

Nothing daunted, we started a pilot project five years ago, making an effort to flesh out the bones of our basic idea. L'Ouverture Theatre project was named after Toussaint L'Ouverture who headed the first black state in the Caribbean in what is now called Haiti. We based it in our semi-derelict premises. The project has gone from strength to strength, proving the abilities of the children and young people, and sharing them with the community through tutorials and classes in dance and tap, singing and music, needlework, woodwork and crafts, and, of course, drama in all its aspects. We have also proved that this style of learning experience can take over where schools have left off. A whole concept of community theatre has now grown up around this and other spin-off projects, with aims and objectives not unlike those of Jesus for his own community. (See Appendix 2.)

We have now developed two computer projects involving parents as well as children, due to the expertise of my curate, Michael Morris, and have others on the way: electronic music making, instrumental tuition, and a printing project, all of which are necessary for the creative arts today but which will also be useful in the commercial sphere.

All that remains, now, is to get the building built to house them all. Although this has been held up in red tape for eight years, we have been offered a glimmer of hope.

The success of our pilot project has proved that inner city people do have souls that cry out for expression and that, given half a chance, they will readily make the effort to help themselves. It has also proved, contrary to popular belief, how willing school leavers and unemployed people are to join in with others in exploring the richness of life which the Arts offer. They gain so much spiritually, and will have encountered lifelong interests and pursuits which may even blossom into careers if the right kind of support is given them.

Brixton, like other inner city areas, is a world microcosm and an exciting place to live. We need to let the positive, constructive and fulfilling parts show through the needs, deprivations and problems of our community because there is a great deal of hope. We must try to live the life that Jesus wanted us to live by ministering to each other, but also by trying to change those things which threaten to hurt or harm us. Just as importantly, we need help and understanding from Christians who live everywhere else, and from those who have power over our daily lives. Only by relating and sharing our experiences will we be able to enrich each other's lives and achieve the fullness Jesus envisaged.

'Jesus said: I have come so that people may have life and may have it in all its fullness.' (John 10:10)

Let us hope that it is not too late to recapture the early excitement of Jesus' followers as they began to realise what he was asking of them. Making a community in which world values were turned upside down and even the wicked were included, cost Jesus his life. Following Jesus may mean being prepared to follow him even to the cross.

Faith in the future, for those tied down by the present,

calls for radical change and the freedom to explore new ways. It will be costly. The change needs to start in our own hearts and minds, as well as in the structures and institutions that inhibit us from reaching fullness of life. It needs Jesus' own kind of revolution.

Appendix 1

Feed The World Service

The disciples said, 'Send the people away to buy themselves something to eat.' Jesus replied: 'You give them something to eat.'

Mark 6:36-7

1. *When I needed a neighbour* by Sidney Carter
   1. When I needed a neighbour, were you there, were you there,
      When I needed a neighbour, were you there?

   Chorus: And the creed and the colour and the name won't matter, were you there?

   2. I was hungry and thirsty
   3. I was cold, I was naked
   4. When I needed some shelter
   5. When I needed some comfort
   6. When I needed a neighbour

2. Isaiah 58:6-11

3. *I have no time* by Bert Jansch

4. Parable of the third world (from *Kyrie Eleison* by Albert van den Heuvel)

5. *Charity begins at home* by Michael Armitage
   1. Hungry people starving slowly, wretched lives beyond our view,
      When the problem's on our doorstep, still we don't know what we should do.

Chorus: Actions speak more loud than words do, we ask God to show the way,
Charity begins at home, but all the world's our home today.

2. Wasted bodies, eyes imploring, hands are begging, empty still:
   Empty smiles and empty gestures will never empty bellies fill.
3. Though we say we love each other, out of sight is out of mind,
   Jesus told us, 'Feed the hungry'—real Christian love is hard to find.

6. A report from Ethiopia and the Sudan (Daily papers or *Christian Aid News*)

7. *All My Trials*
   1. Hush little baby, don't you cry, you know your mamma was born to die,
      All my trials Lord, soon be over.

Chorus: Too late, my brothers, too late, but never mind,
All my trials, Lord, soon be over.

2. I've got a little book with pages three,
   And every page spells liberty—All my trials, Lord, soon be over.
3. If living was a thing that money could buy,
   You know the rich would live, but the poor would die—All my trials, Lord, soon be over.
4. There grows a tree in Paradise,
   And the pilgrims call it the Tree of Life—All my trials, Lord, soon be over.

8. Korean legend.

9. *Feed us now* by Peter Allen
   1. The people came to hear you, the poor, the lame, the blind;
      They asked for food to save them. And you fed them, body and mind.

Chorus: Feed us now, O Son of God, As you fed them long ago.

2. The ones who didn't listen, the rich, the safe, the sure,
   They didn't think they needed the offering of a cure.
3. Yet millions still have hunger, disease, no homes, and
   fear;
   We offer them so little, and it costs them very dear.
4. It's hard for us to listen, things haven't changed at all;
   We've got the things we wanted, we don't want to hear
   your call.
5. So help us see the writing, written clear upon the wall:
   He who doesn't feed his neighbour will get no food at all.

10.   Matthew 25: 34-45

(To those on the right)
Come, all you who have my Father's blessing, and
possess the kingdom which has been ready for you since
the world was made. For when I was hungry you gave me
food; when thirsty, you gave me drink; when I was a
stranger you took me into your home; when naked you
clothed me; when I was ill you came to my help; when in
prison you visited me.

Those on the right reply:
Lord, when was it we saw you hungry and fed you, or
thirsty and gave you drink, a stranger and took you
home, or naked and clothed you? When did we see you
ill or in prison, and come to visit you?

Rest assured, any thing you did for one of my brothers
here, however humble, you did for me.

(To those on the left)
The curse is upon you; go from my sight to the eternal
fire that is ready for the devil and his angels.
For when I was hungry you gave me nothing to eat, when
thirsty, nothing to drink; when I was a stranger you gave
me no home, when naked you didn't clothe me; when I
was ill and in prison, you didn't come to my help.

Those on the left reply:
Lord, when was it that we saw you hungry or thirsty, or a
stranger, or naked, or ill or in prison, and did nothing
for you?

I tell you this: anything you did not do for one of those,
however humble, you did not do for me.

11.   Prayers and the Lord's Prayer

12.   The Offertory: John 6:35, 51, 53-6

13.   The Agape. Everyone shares some bread.
During the distribution of the bread:

14.   *Let us break bread together*
  1. Let us break bread together on our knees,
     Let us break bread together on our knees.

     Chorus: When I fall on my knees, with my face to the
rising sun, O Lord have mercy on me.

  2. Let us pray for the hungry on our knees,
  3. Let us pray for each other on our knees.
  4. Let us praise God together on our knees.

15.   *The Grace*
The grace of our Lord Jesus Christ, and the love of God,
and the fellowship of the Holy Spirit be with us all
evermore.

                                         Amen.

Appendix 2

Theatre And The Community

A. Aims

The Arts provide a unique discipline which offers young people in Brixton a creative security, cuts across class and cultural boundaries and forms a valuable learning experience possibly leading to careers at best, or at least be valuable throughout their lives using their imaginative talents to inspire and strengthen. With the development of microtechnology, the arts and entertainment industries are becoming increasingly important as a major source of employment as well as a constructive use of leisure.

Brixton has many problems but it also provides a multi-cultural environment which stimulates new and exciting developments in many creative spheres.

'The objects for which the company is established are to promote the advancement and improvement of general education in relation to all aspects of the Art of Drama and the development of public appreciation of such Art.'

We aim to carry out these objectives in three main ways:

(a) to establish a Children's Theatre. We believe that it is important to give children experience in the Arts from the earliest possible age.

(b) to offer a work opportunities programme for the 16-25 age group to prepare them for careers in the theatre or allied professions.

(c) to involve the community at all levels with work in schools, community theatre work, and to tour productions in places where people have little access to, or experience of, drama and the arts.

B. Community Theatre

1. History

The idea of Arts for all instead of a sophisticated élite is now common but the idea of involving the community in the production of the Arts—and in this case theatre and music—is only just beginning to be explored. W.B. Yeats' ideas of 'A People's Theatre' seemed only for cognoscenti—an alternative élite—and Romain Rolland's 'People's Theatre' was simply escapist—

'It must first of all give pleasure, a sort of physical and moral rest to the working man weary from his day's work.'

It was Brecht who began the most important work (on *The Threepenny Opera*)—

'1. The fact that the young proletarians suddenly came to the theatre, in some cases for the first time, and then quite often came back.

2. The fact that the top stratum of the bourgeoisie was made to laugh at its own absurdity. Having once laughed at certain attitudes it would never again be possible for these particular representatives of the bourgeoisie to adopt them.'

Brecht's main interest was in debunking middle class values, but it is here that the use of drama in community education begins.

2. Forms of Community Theatre

(a) Impromptu drama, street theatre and happenings are all familiar and can be immediately relevant and political in content reflecting the needs and desires of the community at any given time.

(b) There should be an important place for the presentation of classic drama from Shakespeare to Edward Bond. But the great works of the Theatre must be presented in an accessible way so that ordinary people can share the excitement and insights on life which have made such works classics. It was refreshing to find many who came to our production of *The Tempest*—ordinary Brixton people, usually in the pub and never the theatre—popping their cans of special brew punctuating Prospero's 'cloud-capped towers' and having a good night out.

(c) There should also be local neighbourhood centres for youth and the community to be taught and explore music, drama and dance etc. The Angell Centre will be purpose-built to do this work incorporating L'Ouverture as its drama project to provide for a catchment area of at least 30,000 people in a radius of ½ mile, funded through the Urban Partnership scheme. These centres are most important when government cuts have all but finished music and drama in our schools.

(d) Doing drama for the community using local people can be a source of pride and binds the community together. It is especially important that the cultural resources of ethnic minorities be explored. The use of local dance groups, folk groups, choirs, reggae bands etc. may lead to variety shows and revues, and they can also be used in productions like 'The Tempest'.

(e) Another important aspect of community theatre involves bringing theatre to people in estate halls and local schools. We believe that the formation of a local touring company to take shows to the people would be an invaluable local asset. Our own touring production, *The Storyseller* was written and produced by local black actor, Ronny Cush, and was thought very highly of in many local schools.

C. The Future

1. Several Neighbourhood Centres are already planned and the number of theatre groups will increase. The Neighbourhood Centres should be able to bring their best successes to larger audiences. In Brixton the pressure on the use of Lambeth Town Hall suggests that we need another local theatre centre. The Astoria could do this but will probably be too large. We suggest that the Empress, Brixton's own Music Hall which is still a good theatre and seats about 700 (presently the Granada Bingo Hall in Brighton Terrace), could be used for this purpose. The GLC could facilitate this in conjunction with local firms like Marks and Spencer and other local support.

2. The theatre spawns many ancillary industries like carpentry, electrical wiring and electronics, needlework and tailoring, painting and printing. These could provide training and jobs for many people and the preparations for finding the resources to do all this should be made now.

3. In the longer term the arts and leisure industries, the service industries and education will be the important employers as manufacturing industry becomes more mechanised. The working week may contract leaving a greater percentage of life for leisure or more likely further education/retraining and other courses. We shall need people trained in all branches of the Arts and allied industries if we are to plan for this future in a constructive way.

Michael Armitage

The Angell Centre
Wiltshire Road SW9

Appendix 3

A Statement From Brixton's Clergy

1. We deplore the incident on Saturday, 28th September, 1985, when police violently entered a house in Normandy Road in one of our Parishes in Brixton and shot an innocent woman.

2. We deplore all similar police action in recent times which has sometimes resulted in death.

3. We see no reason why the officer responsible in this case has not been arrested. Are the police subject to a different law from the rest of us?

4. We sympathise with those black people from Brixton, many of them young and unemployed, who demonstrated at Brixton Police Station in the sincere belief that Mrs. Groce was dead.

5. We deplore the actions of those who broke into houses, shops and cars, looting and destroying property. We recognise that they were racially mixed and that they were not all local people, indeed many were simply opportunist.

6. We deplore the fact that police were seen by eye witnesses to be looting in an off-licence and a garage.*

7. We deplore the conditions of life which have persisted and worsened in Brixton since the 1981 riots. Unemployment is nearly three times as high, other statistics concerning deprivation are higher, and few of Scarman's recommendations have been put into effect:

(a) we deplore the fact that no effective steps have been taken by the government in the last four years to alleviate unemployment;

(b) we deplore the increase in real poverty suffered by our people and the subtraction of resources which could have helped to relieve that poverty;

(c) we deplore the lack of attention given to Lord Scarman's carefully and sensitively worked out report.

8. We deplore the lack of concern shown for inner city areas like Brixton by the present government. The government has said that money has been poured into the inner city. We strongly deny this: in fact very little has been given. Even the £25 million referred to was the cost of the Brixton Recreation Centre, funded by Lambeth and the GLC, and opposed by local Tories.

If the Falklands 20,000 people can have £3 million spent on them each day, why can't our 200,000 have at least a proportion of that?

However important the present government may believe its political vendetta with Lambeth to be, it should not hold Brixton hostage.

9. We affirm our delight and joy in experiencing the enhancement of life given to us all by our mixed environment and we maintain that our community has many strengths which come from sharing in mixed racial, cultural and religious backgrounds, all of which is reflected in our churches.

10. We affirm our belief in neighbourhood policing and are pleased at the efforts of the police in this sphere thus far. We ask that the numbers of local bobbies be increased, that their stay in any one area be extended, and that they receive proper respect and promotion opportunities within the force in recognition of their excellent and valuable work. However, we wish the increase in street noise at all hours of day and night from police sirens and howlers be abated.

11. We offer our continued prayers for all those hurt or whose livelihoods were destroyed in the riots.

12. Jesus asked us to help the deprived and the underprivileged.

We urge all those in authority to examine their consciences concerning the unemployed, the deprived, the poor and the needy, especially those in the inner cities. We challenge all those who profess to be Christians, especially those in the government, to put that Christianity into action.

Rev Michael Armitage, St. John's Parish
Rev Lyle Dennen, St. John the Divine Parish
Rev Robert Groves, All Saints' Parish
Rev Tony Lucas, St. Michael's Parish
Rev Michael Morris, St. John's Parish
Rev Dennis Peterson, St. Jude's Parish
Rev Paul Simmonds, St. Andrew's Parish
Rev Maurice Storey, St. Paul's and St. Saviour's Parishes
Rev Barry Thorley, St. Matthew's Parish

* The eye witness has since agreed that what was seen could have been the removal of exhibits following an arrest for theft.

A Statement From Brixton Deanery Clergy

We wish to draw the attention of the Diocese of Southwark to the increasingly shocking conditions of life which persist in our inner city areas, and to those in Brixton in particular. We urge the Diocesan authorities to lead the Anglican Church in following the teachings of Jesus Christ in order to help those who are unemployed, those who are poor, badly housed, and in other ways deprived.

1. We strongly urge the Diocese to reconsider the criteria used to determine staffing levels. Since the *People and Places* Report in 1979, these have been derived, increasingly, from the thinking of the Sheffield Report. However valuable the Sheffield formula may have been for distributing clergy between the Dioceses, we contend that it is *NOT*—and was never meant to be—an appropriate formula for allocating staff within the Diocese itself.

2. We urge that need should be made the primary determining factor in allocating staff, and not the ability of each parish and deanery to pay for its staff. We believe that population should be a principal index of need, and that levels of social deprivation should be taken into account.

3. We urge Diocesan Synod and the Bishops' Council to release the stipendiary clergy places set aside to form a task force, and use that establishment to provide extra manpower for inner city Parishes. Diocesan Synod minutes 1981, no. 3C(e) and no. 4A(iii) should be referred to in this matter.

4. We urge that vocations be encouraged for the inner city; that

indigenous ministries be recognised, preferably by ordination; also that inner city parishes should have greater priority in the allocation of second curacies, suitable deacons or deaconesses; and the licensing of NSMs.

5. We urge that the Diocese support the ministry of its clergy working in the inner city by finding and financing secretarial and administrative help. Financial help should be readily available for Parishes which cannot meet clergy expenses, vicarage repairs, exceptionally high insurance premiums, and other expenses occasioned by living in the inner city. Some have experienced a 200 per cent increase in insurance costs over last year's already high premiums. Many companies will not now quote for SW9 or SW2, and some of our members have been refused insurance because of claims resulting from burglaries. What protection is the Diocese willing to offer? Costs such as these are recognised by other professions. The ILEA, for instance, pays teachers a London Allowance of over £1,000, and 'Educational Priority Areas' are designated where proportionately more of its budget is made available in terms of staffing, resources, and support.

6. We urge the Diocese to provide proportionately more money and resources for inner city Parishes in order to provide fairer shares for our people. In some of our parishes church giving is as much as £3 a head average, among the highest in the Diocese. This is especially significant since our church membership is largely pensioners, the young, the unemployed, young families, single parent families and many living on DHSS and Supplementary Benefit. In particular, we ask that extra specific inner city categories be established under the 'fairer shares' system.

7. We urge the Diocese to support financially and administratively our various imaginative schemes for better use of our church properties, so that they cease to be nightmares of legal procedure, administration, and fundraising for incumbents and PCCs.

8. We urge the Diocese to use the resources of its church schools to help the community by making our schools available as centres for education and recreation outside school hours.

9. We urge that members of Diocesan Boards and Committees,

officers and others in positions of authority, should take the trouble to acquaint themselves with the people of our churches, with their real thoughts, concerns, worries and feelings. We ask them to recognise that many of our committee structures are inappropriate to the expression of those thoughts and feelings. (The participation and involvement of lay people increased considerably once the Brixton Experiment freed us of synodical rules.) We urge others to work for diocesan organisation at a more human level.

10. We urge all church members in the Diocese to take upon themselves the responsibility of challenging central government to be more compassionate, to pour its resources into the inner city, to make jobs and provide better housing and environment for all those living in our inner city Parishes.

We affirm our hope for the Church in the inner city. We believe that because our people are facing daily many of the most urgent problems of this society—so their insights, their lessons, their testimony, have a profound importance for the wider church, in the Diocese and beyond.

Rev Michael Armitage, St. John's Parish
Rev Lyle Dennen, St. John the Divine Parish
Rev Robert Groves, All Saints' Parish
Rev Tony Lucas, St. Michael's Parish
Rev Michael Morris, St. John's Parish
Rev Dennis Peterson, St. Jude's Parish
Rev Paul Simmonds, St. Andrew's Parish
Rev Barry Thorley, St. Matthew's Parish
Rev Maurice Storey, St. Paul's and St. Saviour's Parishes

Further reading

EP Sanders, *Jesus and Judaism* (SCM 1985)
Don Cupitt and Peter Armstrong, *Who was Jesus?* (BBC 1977)
Leonardo Boff, *Church, Charism & Power* (SCM 1985)
Theo Witvliet, *A Place in the Sun* (SCM 1985)
David Sheppard, *Built as a City* (Hodder & Stoughton 1974)
David Sheppard, *Bias to the Poor* (Hodder & Stoughton 1983)
Cortes and Metcalf, *That's My Boy* (Collins 1984)
CK Barrett, *Church, Ministry & Sacraments in the New Testament* (Paternoster 1985)
James DG Dunn, *The Evidence for Jesus* (SCM 1985)
M Paget Wilkes, *Poverty, Revolution & the Church* (Paternoster 1982)
Steve Biko, *I Write What I Like* (Bowerdean Press 1978)
Desmond Tutu, *Crying in the Wilderness* (Mowbrays 1982)
Martin Luther King, *Strength to Love* (Collins Fount 1977)
Robert Clark, *Does the Bible Teach Pacifism?* (Marshalls 1983)
Kenneth Greet, *The Big Sin* (Marshalls 1982)
Ed. Bill Todd, *Voices from the City* (Thames TV 1983)
Ed. Leech & Drummond, *Letters from Seven Churchs* (The Jubilee Group 1984)
Report of the Working Party on Community/Police Relations in Lambeth (Lambeth 1981)
Lord Scarman, *The Brixton Disorders* (HMSO 1981)
Joan Robinson, *Economic Philosophy* (Pelican 1964)
EF Schumacher, *Small is Beautiful* (Abacus 1974)
CH Dodd, *The Parables of the Kingdom* (Collins Fontana 1961)
CH Dodd, *The Founder of Christianity* (Collins Fontana 1973)
John AT Robinson, *Can we Trust the New Testament?* (Mowbray 1977)
Peake's Commentary on the Bible (latest edition) (Nelson)
AE Harvey, *NEB Companion to the Gospels* (Oxford/Cambridge University Press 1972)
JC Fenton, *Saint Matthew* (Pelican 1968)
Dennis Nineham, *Saint Mark* (Pelican 1963)
GB Caird, *Saint Luke* (Pelican 1963)
John Marsh, *Saint John* (Pelican 1968)

Shirley Williams, *A Job to Live* (Penguin 1985)
The Words of Martin Luther King, Jr. (Robson Books 1984)
Mary Benson, *Nelson Mandela* (Penguin 1986)
Ellis Rivkin, *What Crucified Jesus?* (SCM Press 1986)
Kenneth Greet, *What Shall I Cry?* (Epworth Press 1986)
Faith in the City: Archbishop's Commission on Urban
    Priority Areas (Church House Publishing 1985)
RE Clements, *The Prayers of the Bible* (SCM 1986)
John J Vincent, *Into the City* (Epworth Press 1982)

FORGIVE AND RESTORE

Don Baker

When a member of God's family, in this case a loved pastor, goes seriously off the rails in his personal life, the question looms large, 'What should the Church do about it?' 'Is it a matter for the church leadership only?' Should the wayward member be asked to leave or just relieved of responsibility? What should the congregation be told?

This book is a remarkable account of how one church dealt with such a highly charged and emotional crisis. It records in honest detail the ebb and flow of hope and despair, uncertainty and humanity, and relying throughout on biblical principles, it picks its way through a tangled mess to find a place of healing and restoration again.

WHEN YOU PRAY

Reginald East

Spiritual renewal has awakened in many Christians a deeper longing to know God more intimately. Prayer is the place where we personally meet God, yet it is often treated simply as the means for making requests for our needs, and offering our stilted, dutiful thanks. In this practical guide to prayer, Reginald East shows how we can establish a prayer relationship with God which is both spiritually and emotionally satisfying. Through understanding God and ourselves better, prayer can truly become an encounter with God, where we relax into Him, enjoy Him, listen as well as talk to Him and adventure into discovering His heart of love.

If you wish to receive *regular information* about *new books*, please send your name and address to:

London Bible Warehouse
PO Box 123
Basingstoke
Hants RG23 7NL

Name..

Address ....

....

....

....

I am especially interested in:
☐ Biographies
☐ Fiction
☐ Christian living
☐ Issue related books
☐ Academic books
☐ Bible study aids
☐ Children's books
☐ Music
☐ Other subjects

P.S. If you have ideas for new Christian Books or other products, please write to us too!